To Brad & Cindy
Thankyou for
your support &
friendship

Judy Dulouis
Jan. 2009

THE MAGIC THOUGHT

Can't Happen to Me

Judy Dulovic, CHRP

authorHOUSE®

AuthorHouse™
1663 Liberty Drive, Suite 200
Bloomington, IN 47403
www.authorhouse.com
Phone: 1-800-839-8640

First published by AuthorHouse 11/14/2008

ISBN: 978-1-4389-0826-7 (sc)

Printed in the United States of America
Bloomington, Indiana

This book is printed on acid-free paper.

This book was compiled through my own beliefs, values, knowledge and experience gained as a Human Resources and Health and Safety Professional coupled with resources mentioned in this book. I make no warranty or guarantees; only my own belief that if everyone was committed and took responsibility, we could eliminate injuries and illnesses both on and off the job.

Contents

Part III- Health and Safety Key Elements

CREATE A POSITIVE HEALTH AND SAFETY CULTURE

ESTABLISH DUE DILIGENCE THROUGH THE IMPLEMENTATION OF HEALTH AND

SAFETY SYSTEMS

ACKNOWLEDGMENTS

I dedicate this book to my husband Bob, who has given me the emotional support, encouragement, and understanding throughout my endeavors as an entrepreneur and a writer. I also dedicate this book to Howard McWhirter, who coached and mentored me to pursue a profession in human resources and health and safety.

Howard McWhirter: Howard was able to see a diamond in the rough. He was able to set the foundation and give confidence to a house mom who never imagined what her destiny would be. He taught me that I was unable to eat the whole elephant, but if I picked piece by piece, I would reach my goal. Life is no different; if we look at what needs to be accomplished or where we want to go in life, the only way to get there is to sever off a chunk at a time and believe you can do it. He was my inspiration, who had confidence and could see in me what I could not. May he rest in peace?

My husband, Bob: He has been my emotional supporter and best friend, always encouraging me to go forward. He never made me feel like I needed to stop what I was doing and get a regular, paying job. He has always looked out for my internal fulfillment and happiness while encouraging me to finish this book and other endeavors.

My children Lisa and Chris: I thank both Lisa and Chris for supporting me in my endeavors.

My sister, Josephine Martin better known as Jo without the "E": Jo was the instrument of encouragement as I sat on the front porch wondering whether anyone would hire me after so many years. She helped me realize that my skills would come back once I got into the full swing of things. She was right. She has continued supporting my endeavors and helping whenever she can.

Pat DeMerchant: Pat is a very special friend who was always there to listen and encourage me, especially when fear stepped in. That is when you need your friends and family the most. You need positive reinforcement.

Brad and Cindy Whittaker: I thank Brad for reading and critiquing this book and giving me positive feedback. I treasure their friendship and wisdom.

Belanger Family – A special thank you to Jane Belanger, my artist who drew the crossroads to success and leaving your baggage behind. I would also like to thank Abby and John for their support and ideas.

I thank all the people who have influenced my life, both positively and negatively. Without these experiences, I would have nothing to draw from. I treasure the friendships and relationships I have made with friends, colleagues, clients, and participants through the numerous programs I have facilitated. We have learned from each other.

RESOURCES

I have written this book primarily from my own experiences. Those experiences have helped build my own values and beliefs coupled with numerous authors and speakers who have shared the same values and beliefs that I embrace. A few of those authors are:

1. *Management by Responsibility* — *Michael Durst, PhD*
2. *Napkin Notes* — *Michael Durst, Ph.D*
3. *Love Em or Lose Em* — *Beverly Kaye and Sharon Jordan-Evans*
4. *Winning* — *Jack Welch*
5. *Fish!* — *Stephen C. Lundin Ph.D., Harry Paul, John Christensen*
6. *JHSC Certification Training* — *Workplace Safety and Insurance Board*
7. *Practical Loss Control Leadership* — *Frank Bird Jr. and George Germain Loss*

ABOUT THE AUTHOR

 I dedicate this book to Howard McWhirter, who was responsible for the direction of my life. My career started as an Executive Secretary to the Health and Safety and Human Resource Manager of one of the largest scrap yards in the area. I walked into an environment where there were no systems in place and where the frequency of injuries was at an unacceptable high due to no health and safety systems being in place.

After two months on the job, Howard advised that he wanted to groom me to the point of taking his job when he retired. This would require a great deal of coaching and mentoring, as I had never been exposed to either health and safety or human resources. His comment at the time was that I would either love him or hate him by time he was finished with me. There was no doubt that I loved him for his patience in showing me how to manage people and the problems ahead. He became a special friend to my entire family.

At one point I asked him, "What did you see in me?" I was a secretary with no management experience. His comment was that he'd seen someone who was "motivated, caring, determined and willing to go above and beyond what was required." The rest became history as I learned how to get people to understand the necessity of systems. He used to tell me, "You can't eat the whole elephant, but if you take a piece at a time, your mission will be accomplished." I often use this analogy when facilitating groups. It is difficult to implement systems in an environment where you have cowboys doing whatever they want with no rules. By breaking the elephant down, you keep your own sanity, you don't alienate people, and you obtain their respect and understanding.

After embracing his teachings, I moved on to an autocratic environment of "Do it my way or the highway." This would prove to be yet another challenge as I worked through the mentality of "Why change? I have always done it this way." It required patience and trust. I also realized at this point that I needed my designation to give me further creditability as well as an increased pay cheque. My behavior could sometimes be viewed as mothering, because I was the pair of hands, the person that people could talk to, the person who would keep information confidential, and the person who if you surpassed the imaginary line, your services could be terminated in a second. As my sister once said, "If you can work in this environment and make a difference, you can work anywhere." I thank Howard for showing me the way without compromising my values and integrity. Just because everyone around me yelled, screamed, and used foul language, I didn't have to do the same to prove myself.

I continued in this role for a number of years until I was made an offer to work in a participative environment. This move proved interesting, as a floor employee commented he had done a reference check on me. When asked what he found, he pondered and couldn't understand why someone would leave an environment where they were so highly regarded. His perception was that people left their job due to being unhappy or because they hated the people around them. My response was that I needed the opportunity to experience other management styles, and I wanted to grow as an individual.

After a period of time and conversations with many people, I decided to start my own consulting business. I wanted an opportunity to share my values and beliefs on the importance of our most important commodity, "Human capital". I attended a seminar on "How to promote your own business." There was a suggestion to submit articles to the local newspaper. I thought about it and figured there was nothing to lose and everything to gain as I stepped out of my comfort zone.

They accepted and published my first article, followed by ten more on various topics. I learned that if you persevere and are determined, you can do anything. My husband and friends would be my pillars of strength when I got overwhelmed or had doubt. They were there to encourage me and let me know that I could do it and most importantly, don't give up. This is a lesson for all of us: encourage and support loved ones or colleagues when they are attempting new endeavors. When you are out of your comfort zone, you are vulnerable, making it easy to give up, especially if you are surrounded by negativity.

I have since taken the opportunity to write this book as a way of sharing my knowledge and experience on leadership and personal excellence, with an emphasis on building a positive organizational and health and safety culture. I have called my book *The Magic Thought - Can't Happen to Me,* because we sometimes need to wake up and realize that we are in charge of our own destiny. We may have obstacles throughout life, but the secret is to make the most out of it. We have *The Magic Thought* that we will be injury and illness-free, but we continue to take short cuts and think, "*It can't happen to me."* I hope that you will learn the importance of health, safety, and wellness twenty-four hours a day, seven days a week. When someone tells you, "You can't," I want you to figure out how you can. Removing roadblocks is not an easy task, but with perseverance, and if you are open minded and willing to change, it is possible. If something negative happens, attempt to look at the bright side and move on utilizing your transferable skills. Learn from your past instead of dwelling on it.

> Case in Point: *There was a situation where I was doing mock interviews with people who were looking for work. At the time, I interviewed a woman who had been held up at a bank twice. Our challenge was getting her to realize her transferable skills instead of dwelling on her bad experience. Her past was holding her from moving forward. We talked and I asked numerous questions attempting to get her to think positively about the skills she had beyond working at a bank. I was impressed at what I seen underneath and offered her an entry-level position within our organization. At first she was worried she would let me down. It was quite the opposite. She mastered an entry position and gradually moved up to an executive-administrative position. By probing, encouraging, and making apparent the skills she did have, we helped her move on without looking back.*
>
> Case in Point: *There were other incidents where I needed to terminate someone's employment after numerous performance feedback sessions. I always reassured them that although this door was closing, another door would open. Their job was to learn from their past experience and not make the same mistake twice.*

Life is too short to worry about what we are unable to change. It is too short to go on blaming and resenting others. We need to take responsibility, be committed, and be thankful that we have food on our table. We need to look at what we do have. We need to realize that our dreams and aspirations can come true if we are committed and are willing to map out a plan to conquer the obstacles that are holding us back.

My philosophies, values and beliefs are attributed to the journey I have taken in my own career and personal life. Each experience, both positive and negative, gave me an opportunity to learn and grow. It has been through my experiences and listening to frustrations of others that gave me the insight to write this book. I have taken a holistic, 24/7 approach looking at ways to improve an individual's personal and professional life while including health, safety, and wellness. My goal is to assist people in realizing their true potential while staying safe and healthy as they develop habits at home and at work. This will translate into a "Positive Organizational and Health and Safety Culture" as everyone works together as a team with respect, a purpose in life, and an awareness that leads to eliminating injuries and illnesses at all times. We can continue thinking *The Magic Thought – Can't Happen to Me,* but if luck runs out, life will cease to exist the way we have known it.

PURPOSE OF THIS BOOK
The inspiration behind writing this book

This is a book that has been in the making for a while. I was inspired because of numerous managers and employees who were frustrated with the lack of commitment when it came to everyone's health and safety. The common thread through numerous discussions was the lack of support from management and the lack of realizing the consequences from employees. There is always *The Magic Thought – Can't Happen to Me.* I also recognized the close link between health and safety and human resources or investing in human capital. Whether we are looking at our home life, operating a business, or keeping ourselves free from injuries and illnesses, the common denominator is that people need to be fully committed and take responsibility for their actions (or inactions).

I refer to *common sense* in this book because it comes up in conversation and during training sessions time and time again. Common sense was first brought to my attention when I was struggling to think of another article to submit to our local newspaper. It was a friend at an employment agency who asked me to write about "common sense." She would get frustrated, as clients would ask temporary employees to come in and receive minimal training. They would tell her, "Anyone can do the task; it is common sense." After she mentioned it to me, it seemed that every time I had a discussion with a client, "common sense" came up. A coincidence, maybe, but all of a sudden, the light went on and it seemed that everyone was screaming, "That's common sense!" You see it isn't "common sense" unless you have previous experience, skills, knowledge, and training.

Over a period of time, I have facilitated health and safety to numerous groups of employees, managers, and owners. I have found a lot of frustrated people who care and want a positive health and safety culture with zero injuries and illnesses in their workplace. Their major stumbling block is a lack of commitment and people taking responsibility at all levels of the organization. It is common for companies to manage health and safety in a crisis mode. They only do what they have to because a legislated body has lowered the hammer. Employers and employees alike can't comprehend the idea that they can be fined, jailed, or criminally charged both personally and corporately. They can't imagine not being able to look after their family, as they are severely injured or worse still, dead. Organizations are blind to the indirect costs that impact their bottom line more than they realize.

Then there are the employers who have all the systems in place and yet someone still gets hurt. This story goes back to "commitment" and everyone taking responsibility. I am sure we all have good intentions. Is the end result of injury and illness worth it as people circumvent systems causing life-changing injuries?

Case in Point: *I conducted orientation training with an individual whose job included locking out equipment when doing repairs. It was also included during his safety training. Within the same week, we conducted practical training for all employees within his department. Each person was given his/her own lock and received hands-on training on how to properly lock out a piece of equipment when performing work. We thought our basis were covered. A few months later, I received a phone call. There was a crush injury at the plant. This same individual was with his supervisor when the machine was locked out to dislodge some debris from the conveyor belt. Once they dislodged the material, the supervisor started the equipment up. For some reason, the employee decided to run his hand across the conveyor belt to remove some debris that had kicked back. His glove got caught into the roller and his arm was crushed. You have to ask yourself, "How much training is enough?"*

When I think back to this example, I often wander if I did enough. I knew about conducting an investigation, but was I thorough enough. The supervisor was present during this incident and advised he had initially locked out the equipment. In hind site why would the employee go back and run his hand across a moving conveyor with the supervisor present. I second guess myself after 10 years of additional knowledge and experience and wonder if there were other contributing factors that I did not uncover at the time.

As an employer we had taken every precaution in providing extensive training to our supervisors and employees. When looking back, I believe that both the supervisor and employee failed to take responsibility for their actions. They had numerous training sessions on locking out equipment, so what went wrong. This further demonstrates that even when we think we are an expert, there is still room to be open-minded taking responsibility for what may have been missed.

Commitment and the need to take responsibility come up time and time again. We see it in health and safety, as well as our personal and professional life. If we are not willing to be committed to the end goal, chances are that the end goal will not be reached. When we implement health and safety systems, it is imperative that everyone at all levels of an organization take responsibility for health and safety, otherwise injuries and illnesses will continue to happen.

I refer to a "journey" you are about to take, because like anything, there is a journey to get from the beginning to the end. When I assist employers with the implementation of a full health and safety system, it is overwhelming at first. By splitting up initiatives into bite-size pieces, it becomes manageable and people get used to the changes being made. It becomes a journey that when you look back, you can see your accomplishments. Whether it is health and safety, our career, or our dreams and aspirations, the only way goals will be reached is by being committed and taking responsibility completely.

This book is designed to assist each and every one of us to grow holistically in more ways than one. Be open to grow as a person for your family's sake. Be open to grow as a manager or an employee so you can contribute effectively in making the organization you work for successful. You want to strive to be your very best, and most of all, you want to learn techniques in eliminating illnesses and injuries 24/7. Visualize what your life would be like now or during your retirement years if your health failed due to an injury or illness that could have been prevented. What areas of your life will be compromised if you are physically or emotionally restricted from being active and vibrant? We are not invincible. Forget *The Magic Thought – Can't Happen to Me*, because if it does, you are in for a rude awakening. Be open and embrace change as I share my values, beliefs, and concepts holistically 24/7.

ARE YOU READY TO LEAVE YOUR EXCESS BAGGAGE BEHIND IN ORDER TO REACH YOUR TRUE POTENTIAL?

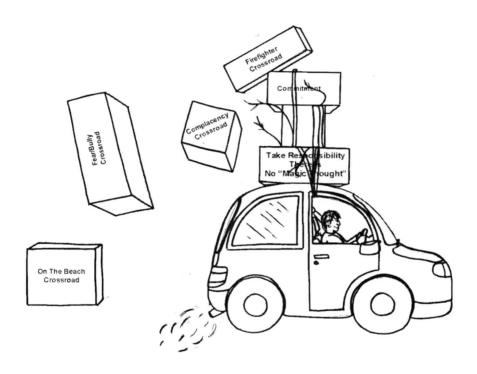

THE MAGIC THOUGHT –
CAN'T HAPPEN TO ME

Why do we have the magic thought that we are invincible?
Why do we live in the past, blame others for our life's destiny, and
refuse to take responsibility?

Injuries and illnesses can be prevented. We have *The Magic Thought – Can't Happen to Me*. It is always the other person. When we fail to take responsibility and be committed for every facet of our life, we fail to reach our full potential. We also risk our quality of life by putting ourselves in harm's way. It is the magic thought that makes it easy to blame everyone else for the path our life has taken.

We drive under the influence of alcohol or drugs with *The Magic Thought – Can't Happen to Me*. There are the university students lining up outside of the nurse's door for the morning-after pill, not taking into consideration that AIDS will impact their life far more than bringing a child into the world.

When we take shortcuts, don't wear personal protection equipment, monkey climb up racking to retrieve an item, or when we perform maintenance on equipment without locking it out, there is always *The Magic Thought – Can't Happen to Me*. There is the magic thought of driving fast, weaving in and out of cars because of our impatience to get to our destination five minutes sooner. Then there are the kids who have fun racing in the streets, only to have themselves or someone else killed because of their irresponsible actions. We can look at any given situation, and I would wager that not one individual who performs these unsafe acts is expecting to be resting in a pine box at the end of the day. I also don't think people realize the impact on their family and themselves when an individual goes through life-changing injuries, not to mention the family agony when there is a death. There is no turning the clock back once the mistake has been made. Is it worth the magic thought as you perform these unsafe acts?

How many organizations include health and safety as part of their budget? How many organizations are prepared financially for the direct and indirect costs of accidents and property damage? As an employer, your job is to take every reasonable precaution to protect your workers. As an employee, your job is to ensure that you adhere to the systems, ask questions when you have concerns, report unsafe conditions, and be safe.

What does it take to become responsible, committed individuals where we look after our health and well-being as well as the people around us? I am not saying, "Don't live and enjoy life." What I am saying is, "Think before you take risks that could impact your quality of life or that of the people around you."

> Case in Point: *As one individual shared with me, she went out to pick up her son on New Year's Eve after a party. Her son, being responsible, made sure he wasn't going to drive home after the party, so Mom volunteered to drive five minutes from home to pick him up. Unfortunately, she never reached her destination because of a drunk driver who crossed over into her lane from the opposite*

direction. As she mentioned, her guardian angel was looking after her, because instead of being killed, she survived—but due to injuries sustained, her quality of life has changed forever. Why do people drive under the influence, when they know the repercussions as they are mentally impaired which affects their judgment, reflexes, and vision? Is it The Magic Thought – Can't Happen to Me?

Why are health and safety measures so difficult to implement? Why do organizations not include health and safety as part of doing business? Why do people in general not take responsibility for their health, safety, and well-being? Accidents causing injuries (and worse still, fatalities) will continue to happen, even with fines being levied and additional inspectors being hired to monitor and enforce our legislated responsibilities. We will continue seeing people killed by drunk drivers or people taking shortcuts. Until we take a holistic approach whereby we create a habit 24/7, we will not change the undesired behaviors that are putting all us at risk. We all suffer from *The Magic Thought – Can't Happen to Me.* The problem is, when luck runs out and it does happen, it's too late. As an organization, our lawyers are asking for proof of training and documentation to prove due diligence. At that point, we realize why it is important to treat health and safety the same as any other part of our business. I find it hard to understand why something has to happen before we come to this conclusion. We place our importance on customer service, quality, and meeting production deadlines, but fail to embrace our most important commodity of all, our people. We fail to protect our people to the best of our abilities. We fail to look at health and safety as part of doing business.

We will take chances without even thinking in our wildest dreams that our life as we know it may be permanently altered. We will continue, with the magic thought causing life-altering affects, until we realize the potential consequences and become proactive in eliminating injuries and illnesses twenty-four hours a day, seven days a week. It needs to become a habit no different than fastening your seatbelt.

This book is made up of three parts. You will journey past the following crossroads in Part I learning the meaning of commitment and taking responsibility:

1. On the Beach
2. Fear /Bullying
3. Complacency
4. Firefighter
5. Commitment

You will continue the momentum as you venture into Part II your "Toolkit for Success." The final stretch of your journey is venturing into Part III, which will assist you in developing health and safety systems that are integrated into your existing management system.

The outcome when you embrace and internalize these concepts is a positive organizational and health and safety culture with measurable results. You will eliminate potential injuries and illnesses as you implement various concepts outlined in this book. As an individual, you will learn the positive affects of being committed and taking responsibility of your life overall. Be open to change, because with change comes growth.

TAKING RESPONSIBILITY

COMMITMENT AT ALL LEVELS OF AN ORGANIZATION

I think I can speak for all of us when I say that we all plan to go to work and return in the same condition, free of injury or illness. Our intention is to enjoy life free of pain and suffering. If this is the case, then why do people continually get injured or killed both on and off the job?

ACCIDENT RATIO

Many health and safety professionals are familiar with the accident ratio model found in the book *Practical Loss Control Leadership*.[1] Take this accident ratio one step further: How many unsafe acts and conditions are overlooked with *The Magic Thought – Can't Happen to Me?*

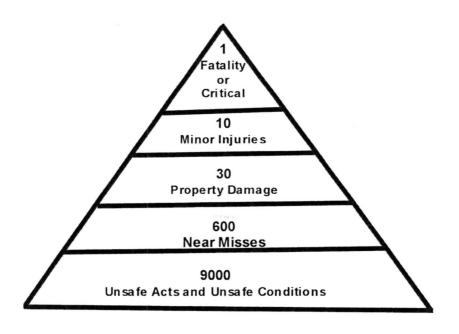

If we recognize, assess, and control the 9,000 unsafe acts/practices and conditions, we can eliminate the 600 near misses, 30 property damage cases, 10 minor injuries, and the one critical injury or death. It is proven that if we control the unsafe practices

[1] *Practical Loss Control Leadership* by Frank Bird Jr. and George Germain – page 21

and conditions, we will eliminate the potential of injuries and illnesses, thereby collapsing our pyramid.

My theory goes past the usual step of implementing health and safety systems in your work environment. I want people to develop a habit 24/7 where they are conscious of unsafe practices and conditions and make every effort to remove those risks. My belief is that if we take a holistic approach in eliminating injuries and illnesses, both on and off the job, we will win the battle against pain and suffering. Once we can master this area, we can continue on the road to promote wellness where we control obesity, depression, heart failure, and other diseases that plague us.

I can't speak for you, but I definitely want to enjoy my retirement years as they creep up. I want to be able to walk the beach, swim, dance, or continue to write. Without my physical and mental health, I am unable to enjoy any of these activities. This gives us all the more reason why we all must pay attention to what we are doing and develop a habit both on and off the job, where it becomes a part of our everyday life.

BEING COMMITTED AND TAKING RESPONSIBILITY

It is my belief that this holistic approach of taking responsibility and being committed 24/7 will grant you success, happiness, fulfillment, financial rewards, and most of all, it will eliminate potential injuries and illnesses, both on and off the job

WHAT DO YOU NEED TO ACCOMPLISH A GOAL?

Some goals may include losing weight, obtaining an education, getting a promotion, completing a project, or attending a meeting.

1. **"Skills, Determination, and Potential"**—Number three on training and knowledge will help in this area, but your own internal motivation and determination is critical.
2. **"Good Intentions" to reach the desired result** Typically, we have good intentions and a desire to succeed, accomplish a goal, and to be injury-free. Our intention, I am sure, is to get out of bed and return in the same physical and mental condition at the end of the day.
3. **"Training and Knowledge"** are gained through education, theory and practical training, and experience. You will also need the physical and cognitive skills to accomplish your goal. This includes having the training and knowledge to eliminate potential injuries and illnesses.
4. **You Need to "Know"** where you want to go or your end goal as well as how and when you are going to get there.

In health and safety, you already know you want your workplace to be injury and illness free. The question is, "How are you going to accomplish that specific goal?"

WHAT IS MISSING WHEN ALL THE ELEMENTS ARE IN PLACE TO ACCOMPLISH YOUR GOAL?

Think of a situation in your life where you didn't accomplish what you set out to do. As an example, after New Year's or before summer, you pledge to lose weight. Most fitness gyms will agree that their gym is very busy after New Year's with committed individuals. You attend the gym and are committed to your goal for the first little while, only for it to dwindle as you get wrapped up in your busy life, putting other priorities ahead. You had good intentions at the beginning, but like all things, it is something you have to consciously work at. You become too busy to work out, too busy to plan your dinners, and too busy to look after your health. Unfortunately, once your health is a problem, your priorities quickly change back to being committed and taking responsibility for your health and well-being. Until you are willing to take full responsibility and have commitment, your goals or aspirations will never materialize, no matter how small or big they may be.

> Case in Point: *I can relate to this as our daughter—a professional personal trainer— struggled with individuals who had good intentions, a desire to get into shape, the knowledge from her coaching, and yet their goal would go unachieved. It was difficult for her to not take it personally. She felt it was a personal reflection on her as the trainer. It goes back to the old cliché of "I can lead the*

23

horse to water, but I can't force him to drink." As
their personal trainer, she could share information
and coach them in attaining their goal, but if the
individual was not fully committed and willing
to take responsibility, the goal of losing weight
would never be achieved. She was not responsible
for the chocolate, chicken wings, and beer that was
consumed in her absence. It is up to the individual
who hired her to take responsibility if they want to
achieve their goal.*

Change in our personal life or in our organization comes only
when we have commitment. We need to be willing to take full
responsibility to improve and change a situation or circumstance
in our life. If you look back throughout your life and thought
about the obstacles that you overcame, you probably agree that
those obstacles didn't go away on their own. You did something.
Depending on the nature of the problem, you had to make up
your mind, take responsibility, and follow through before you
saw the end of it. Think of your personal gratification when you
stepped out of your comfort zone and removed those obstacles.

On the flip side, if you think of events or moments in your
life where you felt sorry for yourself and blamed everyone around
you, the outcome was less than favorable. You existed in your
present situation, did nothing to move forward, and took no
responsibility that you may be the cause. By the same token, can
you think of a time when you or someone you knew was injured?
Were you here in body and mind? Were you rushing, not paying
attention, and involved in horseplay? Were you trained with the
knowledge of what to do? Did you take responsibility for your
actions?

FIRST CROSSROAD

ON THE BEACH
What will you gain from this chapter?

*Recognize how time passes you by as you sit On the
Beach, here in body but not in mind."
See the wonders of a positive attitude.
See how your life changes when you stop blaming and pointing fingers.
See the benefits when you learn from your past,
apply it to the present, and move on.
Recognize how your life can potentially change forever when
you are On the Beach, not paying attention to the task at hand.
You have The Magic Thought – Can't Happen to me.
See how your health, safety and your well-being are
affected when you are On the Beach.*

If you are operating at this crossroad, you find yourself feeling powerless. It is difficult to change or try new ideas. You find yourself making mistakes. The risk of getting hurt is high, as your mind is not on task. You are working to collect a paycheque. Your contribution to the organization's success is non-existent. Instead, you blame management and everyone around you for whatever the situation may be. Your past is influencing your present, and instead of letting the future happen, you worry about what the future is going to hold for you.

It is easy to be *On the Beach* when you want to avoid taking responsibility for life in general. It is easy to look at your past and blame others for the way your life is going. You are focused on the "poor me" syndrome. You look at your life with no hope, and yet you are not willing to identify your obstacles and overcome the barriers or fears so you can move ahead.

> <u>Case in Point:</u> *As a priest once said, "God can't*
> *help a parked car." What he meant was that as long*
> *as you stay paralyzed and are not willing to take*
> *responsibility, God or anyone else is not in a position*
> *to help you.*

If you don't help yourself, no one else can. For life to get better, you and only you must be committed to recognize and make the changes. As long as you feel "poor me, no one cares, or I can't do whatever," you will never move ahead. At this crossroad, it makes it difficult for loved ones, co-workers, or your boss, because it is like talking to a brick wall. You blame, point fingers, and refuse to take ownership. You won't admit that it is you who is responsible for your unhappy circumstance.

As a manager, you tend to operate alone without involving people. You are ineffective with little respect or trust from your subordinates. People who are unmotivated typically do the bare minimum. Your organization is in serious trouble. When people are *On the Beach,* production is low, quality suffers, the potential for accidents is high, and the future of being profitable and in business is at risk. It is just a matter of time before the company goes into a domino effect. Your people are unmotivated, doing the same thing you are; they are simply "collecting a pay cheque."

HEALTH AND SAFETY

BEHAVIORS EXHIBITED WHILE ON THE BEACH CROSSROAD

> ➤ Potential injury is present as you are not where you are. You are here in body but not in mind.
> ➤ Fatigue and constant worry prevent you from concentrating on the task at hand.
> ➤ You participate in training and coaching a number of times without absorbing and implementing the concepts, thus putting yourself and others at risk.
> ➤ As an employee, you take risks by performing unsafe practices and ignoring policies and procedures.
> ➤ You walk by unsafe conditions instead of notifying your supervisor or correcting them yourself. Your perception is "It is not my job so why should I."
> ➤ You are not a team player helping to keep your workplace safe for yourself and others.
> ➤ You are quick to blame or point fingers, not taking ownership when something goes wrong.
> ➤ As a manager, you overlook unsafe practices or conditions to avoid confrontation or additional work.
> ➤ You prefer being anywhere but where you are. Instead of facing the world you prefer to hide. You may be here in

body but your mind is definitely *On the Beach*. You are in your own world with *The Magic Thought- Can't Happen to Me.*

➢ When there is an accident, you immediately play the blame game instead of looking at the root cause of why it happened. You fail to take responsibility looking for other contributing factors.

ATTITUDE

We have choices in life. Choose to be positive.

When you are *On the Beach,* your attitude is usually negative. You tend to blame everyone but yourself for the way life is treating you. We all have challenges and obstacles to overcome. The secret is how we view and cope with the situation at hand. We can look at numerous people who have made a difference in our world with handicaps and setbacks. Their first reaction, I am sure, is "Why me?" Unfortunately, we are faced with challenges in life. Choose to be positive and make the best out of the situation.

EXPERIENCING "ON-THE-BEACH" BEHAVIORS

We ask ourselves, "What makes us function at this crossroad?"

1. I don't want to be here - Think of a time when you were someplace where you really didn't want to be. You are just waiting for time to pass. You are going through the

motions, pretending to look interested, being polite but in actual fact your mind is *On the Beach*, although you're physical body is present. You are looking for the first excuse to leave. This could be your job; a training session you need to attend or someone you feel obligated to visit.

2. <u>I don't like my job, but it is a paycheque</u> – This is an area that many people can relate to. You hate your job, you feel like no one cares so you do the bare minimum to collect your pay cheque. You may be running on autopilot where you have become complacent. In all probability you are de-motivated and have no desire to contribute past what you are already doing. Why bother, no one will notice.

3. <u>Coping with Personal Baggage</u> – Our fast-paced world has put us into turmoil on the personal side. Our highly stressed lifestyles, coupled with poor diet and insufficient time to exercise, creates yet another problem both physically and emotionally. As both parents are working today, it is difficult to juggle both home and career. They are faced with job pressures, university loans that have accumulated, or the sandwich generation of baby boomers assisting their kids as well as their elderly parents. We are in a world where marital breakups and being terribly in debt are part of the norm. No wonder we are *On the Beach*." It gives us a secret place to hide from reality and the pressures of life. If we are *On the Beach,* we don't have to take responsibility for our life's destiny or what is happening around us.

4. <u>Preoccupied</u> – Often we are so preoccupied with our personal problems that we fail to keep our mind on what

we are doing. When this happens, we are setting ourselves up for potential injuries.

5. <u>Physical and Emotional State</u> – We are faced with health challenges as depression, obesity and diabetes has increased. We look at the increase of people taking anti-depressants to help cope with their day-to-day activities. Many employees will take anti-depressants to help cope. Others find that running, exercising and eating healthy is a tremendous way of relieving stress and feeling more energized. As the employee struggles to climb off the beach, many companies promote a healthy lifestyle through balancing work and home, offering daycare on site, seminars on health, or memberships to the gym or a cafeteria with healthy meal choices.

6. <u>I'm not interested</u> – You are asked to participate in a meeting that has nothing to do with you. You go because you were told to not because you want to. You have already made up your mind before the meeting starts to reside *On the Beach*.

7. <u>I'm bored</u> – You attend a seminar and the person speaks in a monotone voice, reading off the screen with no emotion or examples to drive the point's home. I call this, "information dump." As the listener, you can't wait until it is over. You sit there looking at your watch, drawing pictures in your handouts and thinking of all the things you need to do once you are out of the room. You are here in body but your mind has definitely left the room.

8. <u>You're driving down the road</u> – You just missed your cut off as you are driving on autopilot. You have done this drive day in and day out. You swear the car knows the way home as you daydream and think about the day's event or what the evening has in store for you.

MOVING PAST "ON THE BEACH"

AS A PERSON

➢ Choose to be positive. Don't allow others to influence you.

➢ Choose to be here in both body and mind, instead of blaming others or living in fear.

➢ Stop dwelling on your past and future. Enjoy today and let your future unfold in front of you.

➢ Outline an action plan on how you are going to get past your frustrations. Let go of what you can not change and take responsibility of what you can change.

➢ Use positive affirmation statements with a "can-do" approach. Dismiss negative thoughts of "I can't." Dismiss the idea that you can't overcome the obstacles you are faced with.

➢ Be safe! Advise your supervisor when you have concerns or questions.

➢ Follow through when you say you are going to do something. This is a huge trust and integrity issue, when you find excuses to get out of what you originally committed to.

- Embrace a healthy lifestyle of exercise and a healthy diet to provide energy and to eliminate stress.
- Seek outside assistance for areas that you are having difficulty coping with. Ask your company if they have an Employee Assistance Program. The company pays for this confidential program receiving only the bill. There is no information regarding who and what the money was spent on. This gives you access to experts such as marital assistance, financial problems, alcohol and drug abuse or depression. Take advantage of these services. You don't have to be alone as you cope with life challenges.
- Remember, baby steps. You can't eat the whole elephant.

SUPERVISORS AND MANAGERS

- If you see *On the Beach* behaviors, ensure that you have trained and coached sufficiently. This specifically applies when implementing health and safety policies and procedures.
- Avoid placing an individual who is *On the Beach* into high risk jobs where there is risk of potential injury.
- Observe after training and communication ensuring the person was listening and knows what is expected.
- Don't make assumptions about what a person "should" know. What seems like common sense to you may not be for someone else, especially if the person is having difficulties focusing on their job.
- Listen without pre-judging. Look at ways you can assist the individual past this crossroad.

- ➤ Involve the employee in projects or tasks that may be of interest to him or her.
- ➤ Make sure they have the skills and capabilities to complete the project or task you have assigned them.
- ➤ Take personal ownership in identifying whether you are the cause of their behavior.
- ➤ Empower and support your employees' endeavors; give them a reason to come to work.
- ➤ Respect cultural differences without pre-judging. Listen to ideas and act on suggestions.
- ➤ Involve employees in team projects.
- ➤ Silence = Permission! Undesired behaviors will continue if you say or do nothing.
- ➤ Be understanding and sympathetic. Implement an employee assistance program.
- ➤ Set specific, realistic, and achievable goals that will assist the person move past this crossroad.
- ➤ Document and sign off on a plan that you have mutually agreed upon. This holds both parties accountable for making some changes.
- ➤ Be approachable with an open-door policy, so employees can come to you with their concerns.
- ➤ Refer to *Tool 8 and Tool 9* on performance feedback and progressive improvement.

CHOOSE A POSITIVE ATTITUDE

- ➤ Choose to be positive, no matter what you are feeling. Think of people who are far worse off than you.

- ➢ Choose to take responsibility for your health, safety and wellness, eliminating injuries and illnesses.
- ➢ Choose to smile and find things to laugh about—it is truly your best medicine.
- ➢ Choose to be in the present, learning from your past instead of dwelling on it.
- ➢ Choose to be positive to the people around you. Show that you appreciate their endeavors. Don't take anyone for granted. Don't judge and most of all respect each other's differences?
- ➢ Don't give up—Commit to a plan and follow through.

The Journey – Crossroads to Leadership, Personal and Health and Safety Excellence
On the Beach Crossroad
Do you exhibit some of these traits?

Personal Behavior

You are preoccupied with your own problems; finds it difficult to focus.

You are easily distracted, negative, a worrier, has difficulty being positive.

You have difficulty letting go of what you cannot control.

You blame everyone else instead of taking responsibility.

You are oblivious to your surroundings.

You have difficulty focusing on the task at hand.

You feel lost, here in body but your mind is focused on everything except where you are, in the present.

You are afraid to attempt anything new.

You are used to doing the bare minimum to get by,

You commit to something and back out at the last minute.

You are not a team member as you dwell on the past being reluctant to get involved.

You have performance issues requiring constant supervision and coaching.

You criticize the company and people around them. You are viewed as incompetent

You are deceitful and dishonest, does just enough to get by taking frequent breaks.

Leadership Behavior

You avoid setting goals. You find it difficult to hold people accountable.
You ignore employees performing unsafe acts rather than confronting
and dealing with the situation at hand.

You are more interested in your personal situation than the organization's
success and the people around you.

As a supervisor you feel like your hands are tied.

You blame everyone around you when your department is failing to meet
company expectations.

Communication

You are withdrawn and detached, refusing to get involved or participate

You have difficulty listening and concentrating on a conversation causing
you to have instructions repeated time after time.

You are always negative making emotional withdrawals

You find fault and blame everyone else instead of taking personal
ownership.

You can't get off of the merry-go-round. You are always the victim
wanting someone to rescue you.

Health, Safety and Wellness

You are unhappy, depressed, tired, stressed and have a feeling of anxiety.
You are always in constant survival mode.
You are unable to concentrate making it difficult to learn new tasks or procedures.
You are not motivated emotionally or physically so do the bare minimum.

Your mind is not on what you are doing causing potential accidents, incidents, or property damage.
You are often called "accident-prone."
You are afraid to communicate safety concerns.
You do not follow safety procedures, as your mind is not on what you are doing.
You do not realize you sometimes put yourself or others at risk.
You don't think of potential consequences.
You blame others when something goes wrong failing to take responsibility for your actions.

SECOND CROSSROAD

FEAR/BULLYING

What will you gain from this chapter?

You will find out how your attitude affects yourself and others. You will see how your life will change when you accept and forgive others. See the benefits of being positive instead of negative.

See personal fulfillment as you mentor the diamonds in the rough.

Learn to grow and master your fears by stepping out of your comfort zone. See the value of being committed instead of playing mind games and trying to duck out of your responsibility. Recognize Bully behaviors that may be affecting the morale in your workplace and at home.

Recognize how fear and bullying can cause potential injuries and illnesses, both on and off the job.

Recognize what you need to do to transcend this crossroad.

This crossroad has a fork in it. The two forks are "fear" and "bullying." If you are functioning at the *Bullying Crossroad*, then in all probability, your employees are functioning in fear. They dread coming to work, as their environment is filled with tension and stress. These two forks greatly impact our lives, careers, families, and our health and safety. This is one hurdle that many of us have faced sometime during our lives. The unfortunate part is that in many cases, we let bullying and our fears stop us dead in our tracks. We are unable to let go and move ahead as we allow our past to influence our future.

Fear prevents you from moving forward, away from the environment that brings you unhappiness and discontentment. It stops you from progressing or attempting anything new. You continue to sidestep and shirk responsibility. Your life is full of negativity, as you blame everyone for the state of your present job, relationship, or well-being. Your inner fears contribute to being resistant to change or wanting to move ahead. You hate your job, but fear prevents you from leaving and moving on. Your blaming attitude makes it difficult to forgive. You are more likely to want revenge, with the goal of getting back at someone, instead of forgiving them for what they said or what they had done. You become defensive easily. You feel you have to be very protective of your environment. You are reluctant to let anyone give you ideas or suggestions. You are also unwilling to mentor someone, as you fear they will take your job. You are afraid of repercussions or failure when confronting obstacles or concerns. This causes you to keep your thoughts to yourself. You are riveted at this crossroad often due to your past experiences and perceptions.

WHAT CAUSES "FEAR?"

- ➢ It may be due to past experiences.
- ➢ It may be the result of going into uncharted territory or trying something new.
- ➢ It may be that your self-esteem and confidence are preventing you from facing your inner fears and taking responsibility to do something about your situation.
- ➢ It may be fear that keeps you in a job or relationship that is emotionally and physically draining.
- ➢ It may be the result of always being criticized or told you can't do something.
- ➢ It may be that your supervisors or peers are bullies and make you feel inadequate.
- ➢ Maybe no one took the time to listen and encourage you to do what you thought was the impossible.
- ➢ Maybe your goals or aspirations were too overwhelming, so you gave up.
- ➢ You may be *On the Beach* because of your inner fears.

> Case in Point: *I take my hat off to people who have come from other countries, leaving behind a career as a doctor, dentist, or lawyer. They come to North America with nothing more than a dream of building a life for their family that is better than what they have left behind. They are willing to work two jobs and go back to school to gain their profession back. I am sure there is fear as these people make this enormous move. They are giving up everything they have worked for with one difference. They turn over a page for a new beginning filled with a dream, commitment, and the willingness to take responsibility for their future, something that many of us could learn a lesson from.*

41

EXPERIENCING FEAR

<u>Fear of entering a workforce:</u> *As a house mom for ten years, re-entering the workforce, I felt that no one would hire me. My confidence and self-esteem were very low when it came to working outside of the home. I was afraid of going into uncharted territories. Both my sister and my husband encouraged me. They reassured me that the skills I had from before would come back. I had to first overcome my fear and believe in myself; otherwise I would never step out of my comfort zone. My determination, positive attitude and going above and beyond what was required landed me positions that I would never have dreamed of. I was also fortunate to have a boss who mentored, coached, and believed in me.*

<u>Fear of starting my own business:</u> *I started my own business after numerous people had suggested that I work on my own. Fear embraced me, as I feared the unknown. This meant being self-employed, finding my clients, and building a reputation for repeat business. It meant building relationships and helping people solve their problems. My choice of being self-employed has paid off both financially and emotionally. I enjoy sharing my values and beliefs and helping people. Although in most instances, I was determined and positive, I could not have done it without the emotional support and encouragement from my family and friends. This emphasizes the importance of encouraging and supporting people you love and care about in their endeavors. When an individual is out of their comfort zone, it is easy to give up, especially when you don't have the emotional support.*

<u>Fear of Reporting an Unsafe Condition:</u> *How many times do people get hurt, only to say they were*

afraid to say something? I have seen environments where employees were well communicated and positive, and yet for some reason or another, the injured worker failed to communicate their concerns. They may be the only breadwinner, or it may be their first secure job. They want to make a good impression without being perceived as a troublemaker. They fear consequences or looking stupid, or are afraid of what people may think of them. The Magic Thought – Can't Happen to Me creeps up while they think they will be okay. Then the bottom falls out and they are injured. They will tell you, "I should have known better," or "I should have said something." By then it is too late.

You will see through various segments of this book the importance of creating an environment where people can speak up without fearing consequences. This is not an easy task, as people bring with them perceptions, which often are true. It takes a lot of positive feedback, trust, and confidence, as well as communication throughout the organization to set the tone where people will come to you without fear of repercussion.

I share these stories to show you that we all have inner fears. They may be the result of past experiences or insecurities. No one enjoys stepping out of his or her comfort zone, but if we are going to grow, it is a fact of life. I cannot stress enough the importance of supporting and encouraging each other. Whether you are the boss, parent, or spouse, your support and encouragement could mean the difference between success and failure. Reinforce the positive and encourage them to bite off one piece at a time so the goal is not overwhelming. Build trust with people so they will come and talk to you about their concerns. See what it feels like when you have been instrumental in someone's life to reach his or her dream or a goal they never expected to attain.

As a manager, one of the biggest jobs you will have is developing trust and loyalty with employees. Your great communication skills and appropriate body language will assist in eliminating fear. It is imperative that you journey past the *Bullying Crossroad* so fear is removed from employees. You want to create an environment where people can come forward with concerns or problems, asking questions and giving their input.

Fear and bullying is often the most difficult crossroad to move past. You will need to develop a plan in order to eliminate fear and bullying if you are going to operate at the *Commitment Crossroad*.

Never give up or give in to fear or bullying
Learn from your past experiences and move on.

SECOND CROSSROAD – BULLYING

<u>WHAT IS BULLYING?</u> It can be simply defined as repeated and systematic harassing of others. It takes on various forms, such as physical violence, name-calling, threats, intimidation, criticism, faultfinding, humiliation, or instilling fear.

Bullying is the shadow of fear. Throughout life, we are faced with a bully. We see it on the playground when a child doesn't quite fit in. We see it when children play sports. We see it at home when the child is called stupid or is continually screamed at.

If I were to track examples of bullying from conversations with numerous participants, I would be able to write a second book. How many people have walked away from positions because they are tired of the abuse? How many stay because fear steps in to make it difficult for them to make the change. Even with policies on harassment in the workplace, bullying still remains to be a huge problem.

<u>BULLYING AS AN EMPLOYEE OR PERSON</u>—Common behaviors exhibited.

- ➢ You are guilty of name-calling, being condescending, abrupt with no respect for others.
- ➢ You have no patience and are often short tempered or explosive.
- ➢ Your tone of voice and body language instills fear, sometimes without you even realizing it.
- ➢ You are a know-it-all who always promotes your own opinion instead of listening to other suggestions.

> In some cases you may be guilty of calling your child stupid or that they won't amount to anything. This sometimes happens when they are not meeting your expectations.
> You don't give credit where credit is due.
> You are often only interested in your own agenda.
> You make your point through screaming, swearing, or the use of an elevated voice.

BULLYING AS A MANAGER OR SUPERVISOR—
Common behaviors exhibited.

> You are perceived as an autocratic dictator with a "do-it-my-way-or-the-highway" attitude.
> You are viewed as being a bully and condescending.
> Your tone of voice and body language make you unapproachable, while instilling fear in people.
> You tell someone instead of asking when you want something done.
> People are afraid of being terminated if they voice an opinion or make a mistake. For this reason, they will not advise if they see an unsafe condition or feel uncomfortable doing a particular task.
> You have no respect for your employees. You view them as "stupid," "butthead," or "the scum of the earth." (These are some of the comments I have personally heard from managers and supervisors!)
> Perception is that you are too busy or not interested.
> You delegate tasks without ensuring the person has the skills, ability, and time.

- ➢ You are quick to criticize but slow to give positive feedback.
- ➢ You terminate first without prior coaching on the undesired behavior.
- ➢ Your environment is filled with yelling, foul language, and negative connotations.
- ➢ You need to be in control of a situation. You find it difficult to empower people.

IMPACT TO THE ORGANIZATION WHEN THERE IS FEAR AND BULLYING

- ➢ There is low morale. People are unhappy suffering from low self-esteem.
- ➢ Companies go bankrupt because their people are doing just enough to get by.
- ➢ No one cares so quality standards are jeopardized.
- ➢ People are depressed or suffer from anxiety. This results in low productivity and absenteeism.
- ➢ People are stressed and suffer from stress-related illnesses because of their negative environment.
- ➢ Potential hazards are not addressed resulting in accidents, injuries and property damage.

HEALTH AND SAFETY
BEHAVIORS EXHIBITED AT THE FEAR /BULLYING CROSSROAD

Employees put their health and safety at risk because they are afraid of repercussions. The "bully" supervisor will view their employees as troublemakers if they raise a health and safety concern. As an employee, you feel like you are a number and no one cares. You are not empowered or involved in making your workplace safe. Rushing and taking shortcuts is part of the culture to meet production quotas. Your defensive mechanism kicks in, making it difficult for you to openly voice your concerns. Health and safety are viewed as a hassle, instead of part of doing business. Safe work practices are not followed as there is a cost for personal protection equipment, it will take more time to complete the job and in many cases the leader has always performed the task without taking all precautions needed. They have the attitude of *The Magic Thought – Can't Happen to Me.* The management team do the bare minimum when conducting orientation and training sessions. Employees are terminated or sent home because they believe a circumstance is dangerous even though there are laws in place to protect against just that. No wonder we have the perceptions we do and choose to be quiet.

On the flip side, you may be defensive when you are observed and spoken to when performing an unsafe work practice. Instead of thanking the person, you fire back at them to mind their own business. The perception is that you are under attack. As a manager, you are defensive when a government agency identifies deficiencies within your organization. Instead of learning and correcting the deficiencies, you are more inclined to argue or give the government official a hard time. The purpose of their visit is to identify compliance issues with the end result of eliminating injuries and illnesses in your workplace.

> Case in Point: *A friend of mine had an ongoing problem with a safety violation. He advised his supervisor on numerous occasions, only to be ignored. This individual was very familiar with the proper procedures and could see an accident waiting to happen if they continued taking shortcuts. Because he felt uncomfortable and feared for his own safety and the safety of others, he went above his supervisor. His manager acted upon the concern. The supervisor was very upset that this individual went above his head. Out of revenge or reprisal, he gave our friend the silent treatment, and when overtime came up, he made sure he wasn't asked. If the supervisor had listened to the employee's concern and corrected the situation, he would have gained his respect, trust, and loyalty. Instead he chose SILENCE = PERMISSION. He knew there was a violation and he ignored it. His behavior was a bully instead of thanking the employee for protecting him from potential fines if there was a critical injury or worse still a death.*

This type of behavior is frustrating for employees who are attempting to make a difference. It is unfortunate that people need to get defensive and take revenge. If the supervisor were doing his job in the first place, this situation would never have come forward. The supervisor should have acknowledged the employee's concern and taken action without delay. Instead, he chose to do nothing (Silence = Permission) which created the merry-go-round effect of frustration and dissension. As a result, a good employee took an early retirement. Even with provisions in place, employees are often afraid to speak up because they know there will be reprisals, if not now, then down the road. As a member of the management team, it is your responsibility to create a positive environment where concerns can be brought forward and acted upon without fear of reprisal.

RESULTS WHEN FEAR AND BULLYING BEHAVIORS ARE REMOVED

> There is a positive culture where people are not afraid to speak up. In fact, they are encouraged.
> There is no fear, defensiveness, or "mind-your-own-business" attitude.
> People's ideas and concerns are welcomed as everyone works toward a positive safety culture.
> People feel comfortable reporting an unsafe condition, knowing they will be listened to and that the concern will be addressed. There will be no need for a formal refusal process.
> Managers will be receptive to ideas or improvements without becoming defensive.

WHAT IS THE LEGACY YOU LEAVE BEHIND?

What is your Legacy? What will your legacy be when you leave this world? Stand back and look at yourself as a parent, a child, a spouse or significant other. What would your friends and family say about you? If you left your place of employment, would you be missed? Can you take credit for assisting someone to reach his or her true potential through encouragement, coaching, and mentoring? Were you a bully showing little respect for people around you?

WHAT IS YOUR LEGACY WHEN IT COMES TO HEALTH AND SAFETY?

Were you always taking shortcuts, rushing and not following procedures? Did your peers call you "accident prone?" Did you have "*The Magic Thought – Can't Happen To Me*" philosophy? As a supervisor, were you guilty of saying, "do as I say, not as I do," or did you lead by example. Did you perform unsafe actions causing potential injuries to you or the people around you? Have you sustained life altering injuries and illnesses because of the inactions by yourself or others? Most of all, did you take responsibility for your health, safety and wellbeing both on and off the job? Will you be remembered as someone who consciously took health and safety seriously?

QUESTION FOR YOU?

If you were to die tomorrow, what would people say about you?

<u>AS A PARENT</u> how will you be remembered?
➤ Do you balance work and family, always finding time to communicate and be there for your significant other, your children, and immediate family members?
➤ Do you take time to listen without judging or exploding?

➢ Do you encourage and coach your children to be the best they can be?
➢ Are you a role model, encouraging work ethics, integrity, and how to communicate to each other?
➢ Do you praise and support family members, or are you always negative?
➢ Are you quick to criticize before getting all of the facts?

We somehow get caught up with the mindset that we are working long and hard to benefit our family. This will backfire in the end. Don't expect your loved ones to be there for you if you have not set the foundation by building relationships and setting time aside from the very beginning. Learn to balance family, friends, leisure, and work, ensuring that the ones you love the most are not left in the cold.

Lead by Example— How can we expect our children to have respect and good communication skills if they have grown up in an environment of fear and bullying? Is your home life based on an environment of judging, screaming, negativity and outbursts before getting all the details? Have you any idea what this environment does to your children or family members emotionally? When your child grows up and exhibits undesired behaviors, do you ever ask if their environment was a contributing factor? Treat the people around you, the way you would want to be treated.

AS AN EMPLOYEE— What will your employer say about you?
➢ You had nothing good to say about your employer or your colleagues?

- You would not overextend yourself to help others?
- If a task is not within your specific job description, you refused to do it? ("Not my job.")
- You stretched meetings to get out of work?
- You were defensive and argumentative.
- You expected a pay cheque even if you failed to pitch in as a team member?
- You were a know-it-all who has always done it a certain way?
- You refused to change? You always thought you were right and everyone else was wrong?
- You blamed everyone around for your circumstances?
- You refused to listen and be part of a productive team? (Instead, you criticized and found fault.)
- You were always thinking of yourself instead of thinking how you could contribute to your team and the organization's success?

Or will they remember you like this?

- You went above and beyond what was expected and made deposits.
- You provided your supervisor with solutions instead of problems.
- You pitched in and helped where needed, you volunteered for assignments.
- You saw a problem and attempted to correct it if it was within your capability.
- You were enthusiastic when asked to do a task instead of begrudging what you had to do.

- You were willing to learn and take courses to move up in the company.
- You had a positive disposition making people feel good.
- You were open to performance feedback and wanted to learn about areas you may have been weak in.
- You refused to follow health and safety procedures due to your attitude of The Magic Thought - Can't Happen to Me.

AS A BOSS, HOW WILL YOU BE REMEMBERED?

- Were you a bully?
- Were you condescending?
- Did your body language and tone instill fear in your employees?
- Did you explode, using inappropriate language with no respect for your employees?
- Did you mentor and encourage employees so they could master their fears?
- Did people respect and trust you?
- Did they share their frustrations and concerns with you?
- Did people look up to you?
- Did people want to follow in your footsteps?
- Will your employees miss you?
- Did you lead by example from a health and safety perspective

What will your legacy be as a boss, parent, or other influential person in someone's life? Will you be remembered as the person who inspired or the person who instilled fear? Are you full of negativity, always complaining, or do you look at the positive things in life? Do you encourage and praise someone when they do something well, or are you always criticizing?

THE LEGACY OF MENTORING AND BELIEVING IN SOMEONE

As you have gathered from my acknowledgments, my experiences shared with fear, and my personal story at the beginning; my success has been the result of a special person mentoring, believing in me, and making an impression. Howard was my inspiration to continue in my current path for internal fulfillment.

I can reflect back and truly say that although my own drive and determination has been the contributing factor to my success as human resources and safety consultant, I could not have done it without Howard McWhirter's mentoring, coaching and patience as he showed me the way.

Can you imagine the commitment and loyalty you would be developing within your organization if you genuinely cared and gave people under your direction the same kind of influence I was fortunate to have? My experience goes back twenty years, and yet I still feel a profound amount of gratitude.

There are emotional challenges as a mentor. Your biggest obstacle is overcoming your own insecurities or fear. You hesitate to provide too much information, because you fear the person may surpass you. Your true success is when you have mentored someone to enable you to move on either within the company or where you can assist somewhere else. The key to being a successful mentor is the ability to be open and sensitive, to let the person come up with their own solutions, empower and encourage them to step out of their comfort zone. You take the time to listen without being judgmental. You allow for mistakes with the goal of learning from them. You help remove fear as the person ventures into uncharted territories.

Why not be remembered as the person who vastly influenced someone, rather than the person who was pegged as the individual's worst boss? Believe in your people and guide them to move in areas they never thought possible. If you see an opportunity where you can help someone climb the ladder, realize their dream, or become an asset to your organization, the payback is tremendous. You will have an employee who is not only dedicated and loyal, but also an employee who will be an inspiration to others in your organization.

LEAVE BEHIND A LEGACY THAT WILL BE FONDLY REMEMBERED.

DO AS I SAY – NOT AS I DO
LEAD BY EXAMPLE

Do we truly realize the physical consequences when health and safety is ignored at home and at work?

How often have you or someone you have known through your life said, "Do as I say, not as I do?" We have the *Magic Thought – Can't Happen to Me,* as we take short cuts or perform a task in an unsafe manner. If there is an innocent bystander in our mist, whether it is a co-worker, one of our kids, or someone less experienced we say, "Don't do as I do." Your own belief is that you can perform the task safely because you have done it before or your perception is that you will be careful. Up to now you have been extremely LUCKY and nothing has happened.

A supervisor wants to get something done faster so he/she tells the employee, "Don't you do this." A parent performs an unsafe task in front of their children, making sure to say, "Don't you do this, only mommy or daddy can, because we know how."

How often do we take short cuts, perform a task or make the comment, "Do as I say, not as I do?" Throughout this book you are going to hear me refer to 24/7. I truly believe that if we are going to make a difference in health and safety we must take a holistic approach. We also have to make it our priority to Lead by Example and take responsibility for ourselves and the people around us.

> Case in Point: *An adolescent goes camping with a*
> *large group of kids. As the evening drew to a close,*
> *all the kids went to bed leaving the adult councillors*
> *awake talking about the day's event. They decided*
> *to start a camp fire. They were having difficulties*
> *getting it going, so one of the councillors sprayed*
> *insect repellent over the wood. Insect repellent is*
> *highly flammable so he thought this would give*
> *additional assistance to get the fire started. What he*
> *did not know, is that a group of kids were watching*
> *them. Nothing came of it except a few years later,*
> *when one of the young boys was attempting to light*
> *his own camp fire. He got the bright idea to spray*
> *insect repellent on the wood as he had witnessed*
> *before. He attempted to light it without success.*
> *His next decision would result in his best friend*
> *being permanently scarred. He thought if he opened*
> *the repellent and poured it over the logs, it would*
> *then light. There was one technical difficulty, you*
> *never, ever spray or pour a flammable substance*
> *on something that contains a form of ignition. His*

*friend stood back about 12 feet thinking this wasn't
a good idea but before he could voice his opinion it
was too late. There was an explosion which resulted
in his best friend being substantially burned. This
boy's life would be one of pain, suffering and many
surgeries due to a senseless unsafe practice that could
have been avoided.*

*If this isn't enough, my husband and I witnessed
first hand another situation this past New Years.
A group of husbands and kids were ice fishing on
the lake. As we drove up we could see black smoke
coming a few hundred yards from the shore. They
decided to start a fire to keep warm on the lake.
The one fellow poured gasoline over the wood. There
was a flash. This individual was lucky because he
was dressed for winter and managed to drop and
roll in the snow to put the fire out. What is he
telling the kids who were present? I seen dad to it,
so it must be okay. We have "The Magic Thought
– Can't Happen to Me."*

This example not only affected the child, it affected the mother of the child causing her to take time off work to be with her son. The people she worked with, felt her pain and were devastated as well when they heard the news. This reemphasizes my values and beliefs that health and safety needs to be taken seriously 24/7 both on and off the job. It also re-emphasizes the importance of leading by example and taking responsibility for your actions. Imagine how you would feel if your actions resulted in someone being injured because they did it "your way."

Leave a legacy where you can say you consciously took responsibility of health and safety all of the time. Don't be a victim of an unfortunate circumstance because you took short cuts or said those common words, "Do as I say, not as I do." Lead by example by working and playing safe 24/7. Don't let your irresponsible actions be the cause of someone else's fate.

MERRY-GO-ROUND
Are you part of the merry-go-round?

BULLY

- ➢ The bully is the lead horse on this merry-go-round. Some of his or her traits are as follows:
    - o He/she is often condescending using abusive language and tone.
    - o He/she has the "do-it-my-way-or-the-highway" approach.
    - o He/she needs to be in control.
    - o He/she is often negative and judgmental.
    - o He/she typically does not value or listen to other people's opinions.
    - o He/she is usually not sensitive to people's feelings or situation.
    - o He/she is often explosive, easily angered, and short-tempered.
    - o He/she often operates at the *Firefighter Crossroad* being reactive instead of proactive.
- ➢ The bully creates fear, putting employees at risk.
    - o There is fear of being terminated if an individual refuses to do a job due to safety concerns.
    - o There is more interest in meeting production quotas than being safe.
    - o There is no respect for health and safety as it is looked at as an inconvenience.

- o Unsafe practices are overlooked. I call this "silence = permission."
- o The bully will also underplay a potential risk. His/her attitude is that "I've always done it this way, so what is your problem."

VICTIM

- ➤ The victim feels they can do nothing right.
- ➤ The victim feels like they are being beaten up, either emotionally or verbally. Some of his or her traits are as follows:
  - o The victim fears consequences.
  - o The victim feels helpless and trapped in their environment.
  - o The victim suffers from anxiety and is easily overwhelmed.
  - o The victim's emotional state is fragile, with low self-confidence and self-esteem.
- ➤ The victim's health and wellness is at risk, due to their fear of reporting concerns or unsafe conditions.

RESCUER

- ➤ The rescuer is always rescuing people. Although you have good intentions, you are not helping the victim take responsibility.
- ➤ The victim needs to determine the problem and come up with his or her own solutions. You may guide and coach the victim but they need to take control of the situation at hand. This includes health and safety concerns that may come up from time to time.

➤ The rescuer needs to get the victim to take responsibility for their health and wellness without taking short cuts or risks that could jeopardize their health and well being.

People play psychological games all the time. Michael Durst explains it as the "Drama Triangle," where there is a persecutor, a victim, and a rescuer.[2] It is easy to get caught up in the drama or as I call it, the *Merry-Go-Round.* The first category is the bully. Your tone and body language may give the perception of you being a bully. You need something done now. The victim experiences fear as they are dealing with your behavior. Then there is the rescuer, who always feels that they have to rescue people. I have to admit that I am guilty of being the rescuer. The problem with this role is that I am not getting the person to learn to use his or her own problem-solving skills. I am not encouraging them to grow and take responsibility. This is an area that I have to continually be aware of and attempt to improve.

> Case in Point: *The supervisor acts as the Bully raising his voice to the employee. The employee has no understanding of why the supervisor is being harsh. You see, he just got dumped on by his manager. The employee feels victimized as he goes to human resources. The human resources person becomes the rescuer as he or she listens to the problem and makes a trip to the supervisor's office. The merry-go-round has now shifted. The HR person becomes the Bully as he or she approaches the supervisor, who now becomes the victim.*

Can you see how the merry-go-round keeps going around and around? Think of the time and energy lost during this event. If

[2]Napkin Notes: On the Art of Living by G. Michael Durst, PhD, page 97

we all took responsibility for our actions, there would be no bully, rescuer, or victim. Wow! No more psychological games!

HEALTH AND SAFTY

> Case in Point: *If you think of my past example where an unsafe practice was brought to the supervisor's attention, you can see the game being played. Our friend advised the supervisor of an unsafe practice in an attempt to prevent potential injury. When he was unable to get the supervisor to look into it, he went above to the supervisor's manager. The manager initially was the rescuer, listening and doing something about his concern. He became the bully so the situation would be rectified. The supervisor, because of his own insecurities, also became the bully, which leaves the employee in a victim position. The employee stopped the merry-go-round at that point and chose to retire instead of going back to the manager to get rescued.*

THE BANK MACHINE

WITHDRAWAL SLIPS—Are you famous for making withdrawals instead of deposits in your colleagues', friends', and families' emotional bank accounts? Are you filled with negativity? Do you always take from people and never give? Are you on the merry-go-round, in constant turmoil, playing psychological games, always wanting to be rescued or are you the lead horse? How long before people get tired of constant negativity and withdrawals. Instead of making withdrawals as a victim or a bully, turn a new page and start thinking about making deposits.

DEPOSIT SLIPS—Deposit slips are used when you are positive. You give instead of taking. This may be in the form of giving a compliment, sharing a positive experience, or making someone's day. You praise people when you see something done well. You don't take people for granted. You don't assume people know what you are feeling or thinking. You love unconditionally and enjoy friendships, accepting their quirky traits without judging and without jealousy. You make positive affirmation statements, working toward the goals you have set. You are committed to your destiny without blaming others for the state your life is in.

If you are filled with an environment of constant withdrawals, negativity, and "poor-me" syndrome, you start believing and behaving the same. You become negative and depressed as well. I think we would all agree that if there is a choice, we want to be happy.

Think of the person at work making "withdrawals." This is where the grapevine starts as people gossip and talk about areas that dissatisfy them. They can't say or think anything positive about the company or their co-workers. This person is either operating *On the Beach* or they are "complacent." There is jealousy and blaming with no willingness to change or take responsibility.

If we reverse it and make deposits into our bank account, everyone around feels better.

> <u>Case in Point</u>: *I have a client who always says that she is "super fantastic" when asked how she is. She makes the most out of each day and never looks back. She has days like everyone else, where she is anything but "super fantastic" but you would never know it. Although she owns the company, her down-to-earth approach makes it easy for people to talk to her. She is sympathetic as she listens and tries to help the individual with concerns or questions.*

Each of us has problems in life, but as mentioned before, the difference is the attitude we choose. We can choose to be sad and whine about "poor me," or we can choose to be positive. We can choose to make a difference in other people's lives as we make deposits in their emotional bank accounts, or we can blame our past experiences and others for our circumstances. Instead of making withdrawals, attempt to make deposits by making someone feel good. Instead of being negative, be positive and be here now instead of dwelling on your past or worrying about your future.

BENEFITS WHEN YOU MAKE DEPOSITS

- ➢ You will increase your confidence and self-esteem; you will change how you approach obstacles.
- ➢ People will enjoy your positive attitude as you make a difference in the people around you.
- ➢ You will develop trust and respect with people as you refrain from judging and finding fault.
- ➢ Your home life and career will be happy and productive. You will have a "can-do" approach.
- ➢ Your health and safety will be protected as everyone works towards a common goal of zero injuries and illnesses.

MOVING PAST THIS CROSSROAD
FEAR /BULLYING

Map a journey to overcome your fears. Stop playing the blame game. Instead, recognize, assess, and set goals to move forward. Don't procrastinate or think you "can't." Stop looking at life through a window of negativity. Instead, look at life as a new day and how you are going to conquer your inner fears and frustrations to rise past what you are experiencing.

AS A PERSON

> Give up the merry-go-round—take responsibility and contribute as a team member instead of being part of the status quo.
> Look at your bank machine. Are you making deposits or continual withdrawals?
> Stop being a bully: Treat people with respect and show you care at home and at work.
> Learn to forgive instead of wanting revenge.
> Listen without prejudging a person.

- Be aware of body language and tone of voice.
- Be cautious of what might cause you to be perceived as condescending.
- Promote and embrace the idea that each and every one of us has a purpose. We each have our own distinct personalities with strengths and weaknesses to overcome.
- Identify the obstacles that are preventing you from moving forward. If fear or bullying is standing in your way, map out a plan to overcome these challenges. This may include seeking professional help for depression, anxiety, alcohol or drug abuse, or anger management.

> Case in Point: *Get off of the merry-go-round and take responsibility for your life. A few times, I had the opportunity to coach an individual with alcohol abuse. One of our managers had gone through the twelve-step program and was a recovering alcoholic himself. He explained how he almost lost everything before he woke up. We offered outside assistance, but as you know, in order for an individual to do something about an addiction, the first giant step is to ADMIT IT. The next part is much easier, as there are places to go for assistance. It may be a difficult road, but the end result will be well worth it. After months of working with this individual, we were forced to terminate his services. Two months later, he called, asking for his job back. He said that he had lost everything, his job, his house, and his family.*

Recognize that you have a problem, whatever it is, and if needed, get help to get back on track. Don't wait until it is too late before you seek assistance.

AS A BOSS

- Stop being a bully. Be cautious of tone, facial expressions and body language.
- Don't withhold. Praise a job well done and suggest areas for improvement.
- Be positive without criticizing; set goals that can be achieved.
- Encourage and coach those who suffer from fear.
- Coach and mentor the "diamonds in the rough."
- Encourage people to grow and step out of their comfort zone.
- Encourage with positive rather than negative statements.
- Stress open communication without consequences.
- Take joint responsibility in resolving a problem without blame.
- Coach and mentor the "diamonds in the rough." Help them to shine and be their best.
- Empower your people instead of being in control all the time. Implement their ideas.
- Respond to negative attitudes with open-ended questions and paraphrase what they have said, attempting to understand their frustrations and attitude.
- When delegating, ensure that the person has the time and the skills to complete the task.
- Create an environment where health and safety are paramount.
- Remove fear and bullying barriers that cause people to not report hazards or injuries.

The Journey – Crossroads to Leadership, Personal and Health and Safety Excellence
Fear/Bully Crossroad
Do you exhibit some of these traits?

Personal Behavior

Fear

You fear rejection when giving your opinion. You lack loyalty, as you fear to get too involved with team members.

You fear failure and so resist trying something new. You guard information or knowledge you have come across.

You have fear from past experiences prevents you from moving forward, you avoid challenging activities.

Your fear makes life overwhelming, you refrain from taking initiative.

Bully

You are viewed as an authoritarian, confrontational, negative and you are closed-minded.

You are self-centered using aggressive behaviors. You have difficulty agreeing with the opinions of others,

You have difficulty listening as you have already formed your own opinion or answer before the other person is finished.

You are a "know it all" and will circumvent procedures where possible.

You are unconcerned with the negative you make in people's lives. You enjoy criticizing failing to praise.

You have an attitude, "If you don't like it, leave," or "Do it my way or the highway."

Leadership Behavior

Fear

Fear stops you from making changes that could improve the operation.

Fear prevents you from effectively coaching and mentoring people to progress in the organization.

Fear prevents you from going after future promotions.

Bully

You use a dictatorship approach with your condescending, unapproachable, quick to criticize behavior.

You view staff as being lazy because they may not have the same work ethics as you.

You fail to consider a person's workload and their ability to perform the task before you delegate.

You do not encourage creativity, decision-making or coming up with ideas to problems.

You must always be right and you won't admit when you are wrong.

You lose control before getting all the facts.

Your undesired behavior makes it difficult for people to be dedicated or loyal.

Communication

<u>Fear</u>

You are negative and can't get off the merry-go-round. Your perception is that no one will listen to you.

You are quiet and withdrawn afraid to voice your opinion.

<u>Bully</u>

You tell instead of involving staff, people have no respect, loyalty or trust for you.

Your body language, tone of voice and communication skills makes you unapproachable

Your abusive language coupled with your short temper and explosive attitude instills fear to those around you.

You are the bully on the merry-go-round, causing grief to people around you.

Health, Safety and Wellness

<u>Fear</u>

You suffer from insomnia, headaches, and could be prone to depression or anxiety. You worry and feel victimized.

You are afraid to advise when you see an unsafe condition. You don't ask questions when you have a concern.

<u>Bully</u>

You are prone to heart failure, high blood pressure and have an elevated stress level.

You make communication difficult so people don't talk to you about health and safety concerns.

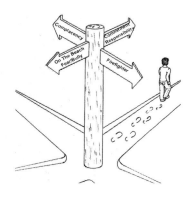

THIRD CROSSROAD

COMPLACENCY

What will you gain from this chapter?

We will address the cost to an organization when people are de-motivated. We will address how to motivate people. We will look at how your values and beliefs affect your behavior.
We will learn how "Complacency" and a lack of willingness to change can impact your health and well-being. We will learn how to transcend past this crossroad.

This is an area where you resist change and being flexible. If you are sitting at the *Complacency Crossroad*, you are not willing to try something new. You are caught in a rut. You let time pass you by. You have accepted your path in life. One day runs into the next as you stick to the same schedule. It is easier to follow others and be part of the crowd, instead of taking the initiative to move past this crossroad. It is easy to be complacent, because you can hide or stick your head in the sand so you never face your true potential. It may be fear, a bully or circumstances beyond your control that stop you from moving forward.

If you have been in the same job for a number of years, you are settled and are unwilling to change the way it has always been done. You are closed-minded to change or learning anything new, as it will interfere with your day-to-day routine. This crossroad can seriously impact an organization, as we will see in the next chapter. If organizations are going to survive in this competitive global market, both management and employees must be willing to make changes; otherwise, you will stay in the same rut, as other companies take over your market share.

> Case In Point: *I can think of a company on the verge of bankruptcy. Their employees were content collecting their paycheque doing the bare minimum. They would take short cuts and not follow safety procedures. They had always done it this way, so why change. If you were somewhat motivated, you were soon told by your colleagues to stop before you made everyone look bad. They blamed management for the state of the company taking no responsibility of their own.*
>
> *I look at this scenario and ask myself, "What went wrong?" First of all, there was no accountability on either the employees or supervisor's part. There was a lack of leadership and direction. They failed to include their employees and raise the bar on required expectations. They also didn't provide incentives to encourage people to work beyond the status quo. It was a toxic environment of blaming each other with the Merry Go Round affect instead of working together to figure out their problems. Is it the magic thought that we are guaranteed a paycheque and a pension without working 100%? We've always done it that way in the past, so the cash cow should just continue giving us money*

without us actually earning it. How many people are out of work due to bankruptcy, only to blame everyone else but themselves?

As a manager, at this crossroad, you are looked at as a morale booster while supporting staff. You don't push for results. You are content letting everyone do what has always been done. You never raise the bar. You tend to overlook unacceptable behaviors or work not being performed. It is easier to turn a blind eye than to confront people. As long as no one is holding you accountable, there is no reason for you to rock the boat. The problem when you manage your department at the *Complacency Crossroad* is that you create inconsistencies within the organization as other managers operate at the *Commitment Crossroad*, where they hold their people accountable.

HEALTH AND SAFETY
BEHAVIORS EXHIBITED AT THE COMPLACENCY CROSSROAD

As a manager, you tend to overlook unsafe acts or conditions. You do not lead by example. You do not wear personal protection equipment or follow safe work practices. Employees are no different, as there is no one setting and enforcing the procedures that have been communicated. It becomes difficult when the organization implements a health and safety system where you must adhere to policies and procedures. You and others are resistant. You want to continue performing unsafe practices with *The Magic Thought – Can't Happen to Me.* You are an accident waiting to happen as you take shortcuts and ignore safe operating procedures. You fail to understand that these undesired behaviors will in time put you and others around you at risk. Up to now, you have been extremely LUCKY.

SILENCE = PERMISSION

This phrase can be used to relate to situations 24/7. If we allow shortcuts or ignore safe operating procedures, then we are giving permission to act in an unsafe manner. The same holds true for our kids. If we are silent when they exhibit an undesired behavior, the message we are sending is that their parents don't care or it's okay—otherwise they would have said something. There is no accountability.

MOVING PAST THIS CROSSROAD
COMPLACENCY

AS A PERSON

- Don't be a creature of habit. Step out of your comfort zone to meet new challenges.
- Instead of giving your boss a problem, think of a solution.
- Don't be part of the status quo. Make a difference at work and at home.
- Be open-minded.
- Commit to continuously learn. In today's competitive and technological world, it is a fact of life.
- Be open to change.
- Take on new challenges without always expecting something in return.

> Case in Point: *There are many people who started off in a very junior position. They went above and beyond what was expected. Their hard work paid off as they climbed the corporate ladder. They learned the business from the ground up giving them an understanding of the operations as well as earning respect from their employees. They maintain an attitude that they won't have someone do a task that*

they personally would not do themselves. If we were to talk to a number of successful people, it did not just happen. Chances are they worked hard to get where they are today.

➤ Be where you are both in body and in mind. Don't revert to being *On the Beach*. It is anti-productive and puts people at risk as you are not where you are.

➤ Change your tasks where possible to eliminate routine work.

➤ Don't be so confident or complacent that you fail to follow safe operating procedures or wear personal protection equipment.

AS A BOSS

➤ Involve people and get them to see the benefit of operating at the *Commitment Crossroad*.

➤ Communicate the importance of continuous learning and being able to adapt to change.

➤ Utilize people's talents so they stay motivated.

➤ Evaluate, coach, and mentor your people on an ongoing basis.

➤ Set up teams to problem solve encouraging employees to contribute.

➤ Inspire positive attitudes and set objectives and goals to reach.

➤ Nurture and encourage ideas for improvements. Don't be the rescuer.

➤ Create an environment where people can learn from their mistakes.

- Communicate and train on policies and procedures.
- Delegate and ensure the person has the skills, abilities, and time to complete the task.
- Hold people accountable for their actions.
- Let them know your expectations.
- Let people know the consequences for not meeting your expectations.

IMPROVING HEALTH AND SAFETY

- ➤ Silence = Permission is not acceptable.
- ➤ Develop and implement safe operating procedures on major tasks.
- ➤ Hold people accountable to ensure they follow safe practices with no shortcuts.
- ➤ Communicate and train on expectations followed with performance appraisals.
- ➤ Observe employees and coach or discipline when unsafe practices are being performed.
- ➤ Conduct regular safety talks to raise awareness. Get employees to buy in to ideas.

WHAT IS THE COST OF BEING DE-MOTIVATED

First Phase of Employment Placement— When you hire an individual, they are motivated and excited they landed the job they applied for. They have to go through a learning curve before they are fully competent. You have ensured they have the skills, knowledge, and ability to perform their job. You have made allowances for training and bringing them up to speed on the requirements of the particular job they have just been hired to do.

Second Phase of Employment Placement— This employee is now competent, as they understand your expectations. They are still motivated and excited about the job they have accepted. Unfortunately, the excitement quickly wears off, sending the employee into phase three (competent but de-motivated). The skills, abilities, and knowledge of the operations are present, so why do they become de-motivated?

Third Phase of Employment Placement— The employee is still competent but de-motivated. What is the cost to the organization at this point? What causes your employee to fall into this phase? Chances are, they are not alone, because as we know, when a group of employees is within a certain status quo, they will recruit others to join them. This group is not only de-motivated, but you have the rumor mill and dissension. This means that everyone is doing just enough to meet expectations.

I have seen situations where an employee sitting in phase two is highly motivated. Unfortunately, this motivated employee is faced with criticism from his/her fellow employees who are sitting in phase three or four. They don't want to look bad, so they discourage and make life miserable for our phase two employee.

How long will it take before this individual gives up and joins the rest?

Fourth Phase of Employment Placement—The employee soon moves from phase three to phase four (not competent and de-motivated). They are *On the Beach* at this point. They are not only de-motivated, they are non competent. They don't care what happens. You are in big trouble, if your employees are residing in phase four.

The new generation is educated, wants to make a difference, and wants to be recognized. Your success depends on change that will motivate your employees to remain in phase two. Are you struggling as an organization? If so, ask yourself, "What phase do most of your employees fall into?"

As time goes by, you will find it more and more difficult to find qualified motivated employees to fill the shoes of those who have left or are presently working in phases three and four. Invest in human capital like you have never done before. They are your lifeline to longevity. Recognize, identify, and implement a plan to pull your people back into phase two.

> Case in Point: *If I relate back to the previous story, the leadership team would have to take drastic measures to get their people out of phase four and out of being complacent if they were going to profit as an organization. One of the new strategies was to give employees incentives for work performed. They also provided funding for equipment and resources.*
>
> *How quickly people moved into phase two. For years, there was nothing to motivate employees. If only the original management team had realized that including employees in the process, getting their*

buy in and rewarding them for their efforts would
give them the results they needed.

As I keep saying, "invest in human capital." They
are your lifeline.

WHY EMPLOYEES DRIFT
FROM PHASE TWO TO PHASES THREE AND FOUR

I have outlined below some reasons why employees move out of phase two. They are as follows:

➤ The person was misled on career opportunities that were promised.

➤ There is no stimulation. The person is bored doing the same thing over and over.

➤ You hired the wrong person for the job.

➤ The person is either over qualified or under qualified. This means they are either bored or overwhelmed.

➤ There is an environment filled with fear and bullying.

➤ Promises are not kept.

➤ There is no appreciation for work performed.

➤ There is no positive feedback letting employees know when they do well.

➤ There is no encouragement.

➤ No one cares about the employee's health and well-being.

➤ Production is put ahead of health and safety.

➤ Employees are overworked and underpaid.

➤ There is no career growth.

➤ There are no incentives or rewards for giving 100%.

> <u>Case in Point:</u> *As the book* Love 'Em or Lose
> 'Em *points out, "the top reasons why employees*

stay at a company is career growth, learning and development, exciting and meaningful work, a challenge, making a difference and working with a great team of employees. Money and benefits was listed as eleventh."[3]

COST OF BEING COMPETENT BUT DE-MOTIVATED

1. Employees get careless and do not pay attention causing potential injuries.
2. Accidents happen as people refuse to follow safe operating procedures. They prefer the way they have always done it. It's that *Magic Thought – Can't Happen to Me.*
3. Shortcuts are taken.
4. Increased property and product damage occurs, because employees don't care.
5. Employees get frustrated and angry, which generates verbal abuse and violence.
6. There is increased absenteeism.
7. Employees do the bare minimum to collect their pay cheque.
8. Employees tend to point fingers and blame others instead of taking personal responsibility.
9. Employees feel no one cares and no one wants to listen.
10. Opinions are not valued so great ideas are not shared.
11. Housekeeping is an issue as employees are de-motivated to clean up.
12. Quality is compromised.
13. Employees work for a paycheque without contributing to the success of an organization.

---

[3] *Love 'Em or Lose 'Em – Getting good people to stay* by Beverly Kaye and Sharon Jordan-Evans

14. There is low productivity as people do the bare minimum.

15. New employees move into phase three quickly as they are influenced by disgruntled non-performers.

16. If an unsafe condition is observed, nothing is said, due to the view that no one will listen or fix it.

17. Lastly, if you continue down this path, don't be surprised if you end up going bankrupt. You need your people motivated and competent more than you can ever realized.

MOTIVATE EMPLOYEES WITH BOTTOM-LINE RESULTS

Invest in Human Capital—The payback far exceeds the investment.

Companies are able to market their product, provide quality and service, and yet something is missing for them to be successful. The missing link is an investment in human capital. The top 100 companies to work for all have innovative ways of motivating and making their staff feel special.

THE PAYBACK

➢ Employees remain in Phase two, and are competent and motivated.

➢ Higher productivity occurs when employees are happy and feel appreciated.

➢ Retention with turnover is minimized because employees enjoy their job.

- ➢ There are fewer accidents.
- ➢ A sense of loyalty and a positive environment is created.

EMPLOYEE PERKS:

- ➢ An onsite, free fitness club with personal trainers promotes health and fitness, resulting in less stress, more energy and reduced.
- ➢ Membership to the local gym encourages health and wellness.
- ➢ Additional days off can be used for sick days, doctor's appointments, or their kids' activities.
- ➢ An onsite day care means no worry or searching for a safe and fun place for babies and toddlers.
- ➢ Increased vacation, including personal days, is offered.
- ➢ Bonuses, incentives, profit-sharing, extended medical or contributions toward employee pension plans.
- ➢ Educational courses are paid for by the company resulting in people obtaining their designation in their field of expertise.
- ➢ Seminars on wellness, investing, and other areas of interest are offered.
- ➢ Free trips are given when goals are achieved.
- ➢ Team games such as baseball, hockey, or curling are organized.
- ➢ Provide family functions—Christmas party, summer barbecue, family picnic, golf tournament, Easter egg hunt, etc.

OTHER WAYS TO MOTIVATE STAFF

- ➢ Hiring—Set employees up for success from the very beginning. When assessing someone's potential, ensure that they have the skills, knowledge, and capability to perform the job. Be prepared to train or accommodate the individual in areas they are not qualified to do.
- ➢ Give fair market value pay for the job being performed.
- ➢ Share your vision and mission and include them in the process.
- ➢ Show you care by providing a safe and healthy environment.
- ➢ Create a positive culture where there is open communication.
- ➢ Listen and encourage ideas from staff.
- ➢ Create a culture of respect and caring.
- ➢ Empower employees to make decisions.
- ➢ Delegate effectively to ensure that the person is capable of doing the task.

The Journey – Crossroads to Leadership, Personal and Health and Safety Excellence
Complacency Crossroad
Do you exhibit some of these traits?

Personal Behavior

You are resistant to change, communication exists through the rumor mill or grapevine of gossip.

You are stereotyped, hesitant to try anything new and quite content in your present situation.

You have great people skills, you want to be liked, and dislike hurting people's feelings.

You are often unreliable missing deadlines.

You take extended breaks and lunches.

You are seldom held accountable for your actions. Your supervisor allows this behavior. (silence=permission)

You don't want to rock the boat.

You are content with your life and believe there is no other way.

You have always done things a specific way.

You feel victimized when required to make changes.

You are part of the status quo of "Competent/de-motivated."

You go through the motions day in and day out.

You have accepted your life the way it is, with no desire to improve or progress.

Leadership Behavior

You are very accommodating.

Building relationships is very important to you.

Staff needs to be protected so you are the rescuer on the merry-go-round.

You are reluctant to exercise power.

You are viewed as indecisive and inconsistent.

You seldom delegate

You are unable to assign realistic priorities or give direction.

Others are interfering when there is a disagreement. You hate conflict and blame the other person.

You are hesitant and shy.

You seldom push for results. Instead you are laid back, it can wait for tomorrow.

You don't hold people accountable.

You are unresponsive to change.

You are not willing to pitch in to raise the bar for a more productive environment.

You refrain from disciplining your people preferring Silence = Permission.

Communication

It is very important emotionally to be liked by the people around you. You are generally positive.

You dislike negative feedback, you feel you are being picked on, has difficulty understanding why it is necessary to change.

You are a relationship builder who thrives on positive relationships.

You refrain from giving honest feedback when a person is not meeting expectations.

You are more concerned with protecting relationships than scolding violators for safety infractions.

Health, Safety and Wellness

You live in *The Magic Thought – Can't Happen to Me.* "Why change, life is good"

You follow everyone else ignoring safety.

You have always done a task a certain way so won't adapt safety precautions. "Nothing has happened up to now, so why change?" This behavior will continue unless you are held accountable for your actions.

FOURTH CROSSROAD

FIREFIGHTER

What will you gain from this chapter?

Realize the physical and mental stress when you are continually firefighting.
Learn the benefits of setting realistic expectations while effectively delegating to others.
See the advantages of being proactive instead of reactive.
Recognize how rushing, taking shortcuts, and making quick decisions can affect health and safety and business decisions. Learn how to transcend this crossroad.

At the *Firefighter Crossroad*, you are often under a lot of pressure, some of which is self-inflicted. You are a high achiever who is goal-oriented and highly internally motivated. This causes you to put extra pressure on yourself and others. You find yourself being reactive instead of proactive in many situations. You make snap decisions or judgments where you "act first and worry later." You are viewed as being aggressive and out for your own personal gain. Your impatience sometimes creates confusion and frustration for others. This sometimes leads to shortcuts and injuries. You have many positive traits. You are committed, organized, and you are a good communicator. The negative side is that you pre-judge because you want everyone to think and be like you. You want everyone to have your work ethics, drive, and determination. If you are not careful, the stress of pushing yourself could result in heart failure.

> Case in Point: *A general manager of a big-box store was ready to find another job because he was the Firefighter. It drove him crazy managing people who did not have the same work ethics and motivation that he had. They didn't care, would think nothing of taking a day off or coming in late, and would never go beyond what was expected. He was tired of babysitting and trying to motivate these individuals to take pride in their work.*
>
> *At one point, he asked if I knew of anyone looking for a senior general manager. He had enough. My comment was that the problems and frustrations he was experiencing would be the same no matter where he went. People are people. He wanted his staff to work and think like he did. He wanted them to have good work ethics and to take initiative. His challenge was getting his staff off the beach, out of Complacency, and definitely out of Phase Three or Four.*

This takes a lot of work on a manager's part to help people realize what their purpose is. Sometimes their perception is one of discontentment and unhappiness because they feel they deserve more. Sometimes people think others are lucky to be in a particular position; not realizing the hard work and commitment it took to climb the corporate ladder. As a mentor and coach, you need to instill your values and expectations to let employees know that this isn't the end of the road, but a building block for future opportunities. Encourage employees to think positively and to make deposits into their bank accounts. Get them to map out their own journey for their future, making the best out of the here and now.

As a *Firefighter,* how often do you fail to think through a situation or problem? How much time and money is wasted with quick decisions? Are you a know it all who fails to ask employees for their input? Sometimes, we are so intent in what we want to accomplish, we fail to ask others. Don't underestimate what people on the floor may know. Be receptive to their ideas.

> <u>Case in Point:</u> *I had a situation where a furnace was being built for melting ingots. They had to retrofit it after the fact to accommodate skimming the heat. An older operator commented, "Why didn't they ask me? I would have told them it wasn't going to work."*

Ask yourself if your goals are too aggressive. Are you walking over people to get to your destination? Is your life comprised of all work and no play? What price are you willing to pay? Once you reach the top, are the people you love going to be waiting for you?

HEALTH AND SAFETY

BEHAVIORS EXHIBITED AT THE FIREFIGHTER CROSSROAD:

Health and safety is at risk for the following reasons:

- ➤ Band-Aid approach is used instead of being proactive.
- ➤ You fix the immediate problem instead of looking for the root cause.
- ➤ Due to impatience to get things done, people take shortcuts or rush.
- ➤ There is an assumption that people should know: "It is common sense!"
- ➤ Snap decisions are made without addressing potential health and safety risks.
- ➤ Safety is not considered when timelines are set.
- ➤ Goals are set without involving the Joint Health and Safety Committee.
- ➤ You ignore policies and procedures to complete the task at hand.

Problem vs. Solution -Do you ask for a solution or do you accept and fix the problems presented to you? You may sometimes think it is easier to do it yourself, but in actual fact, when you give it back to the person, it holds them accountable to come up with a solution. From a time-management perspective, it should help your workload, but most of all, it makes the employee think and act before coming forward. This builds trust and shows you value their opinion.

> Case in Point: *This is an area I have had to work at. My brain is wired to look at the problem and come up with a solution. As a human resource manager, I have to admit I was the Firefighter. It seemed like I was always putting out fires. If a manager or supervisor came to me with a problem, I automatically either fixed it or gave a couple of options on what to do. I was guilty of the same thing at home. If our daughter had a problem, I would kick into the "fix-it mom" mode. I would give her a few options and we would discuss the pros and cons. I should have been their sounding board or coach to help them decide on the best option by listening and asking open-ended questions on how to solve the problem. I should have asked them to look into it further coming up with some solutions on their own before coming to me. This way, it would have been their idea and they would have taken full responsibility for it.*

MOVING PAST THE FIREFIGHTER CROSSROAD

1. **Crisis Management**—Stop being a *Firefighter*. Don't wait for a crisis; be pro-active. Set realistic goals, weighing all variables.

2. **High Expectations**—Not everyone is internally motivated like you. This gives you a great opportunity to mentor an individual on the benefits when you go above and beyond. You need to get them excited and see "what's in it for them." This requires a lot of patience and understanding.

3. **Reactive Instead of Proactive**—Put systems in place to anticipate business challenges. When there is an accident, correct the root cause instead of using a band-aid approach. Eliminate the hazard at the source if feasible. Be farsighted instead of nearsighted. It may cost you more in the beginning, but look at the savings over the long term.

4. **Slow Down and Prioritize** what you need to get accomplished. Identify what you and your team can realistically achieve within a reasonable timeframe. Learn to say no if it is impossible without obtaining additional help and resources. If you are making health and safety recommendations, rate the hazard A, B, C, or D, ensuring that "A" hazards are corrected immediately.

5. **Don't Make Snap Decisions**—Sometimes decisions are made without thinking things through. Look at various options and empower people to problem-solve and provide you with solutions to the problem at hand. Look at how much time is required, who will be affected, what other obstacles may be created, and whether it will be a short- or long-term fix.

6. **Setting Unreasonable Timelines**—If you are in a crisis mode, it is sometimes necessary to set timelines that are difficult to achieve. This puts undue stress on you and others as you scramble to get the task at hand done. There is also the potential of injury as people take shortcuts, rush, and don't think things through. Promote the idea of being proactive instead of reactive, so realistic timelines can be set with resources and manpower to accommodate the workload.

7. **Impatience**—Impatience can cause you to be reactive instead of proactive. It also causes people to rush and take shortcuts, which can put them at risk. Ensure that you have properly planned and allowed enough time in an attempt to eliminate your impatient behavior.

8. **Empower People**— You may have some work ahead empowering people instead of taking the whole world into your own hands. When someone comes to you with a problem, ask them for a solution. Give them an opportunity to problem-solve instead of doing all of the work yourself.

9. **Fail to Delegate Effectively**— Your first task is to let go and effectively delegate. In doing that, you want to make sure the person has the skills, ability, and time to accomplish

the project. Your impatience will make it tempting to take the task back. Instead, give the person time to learn and become competent as you when performing the task assigned.

10. **Assume Common Sense**— We sometimes assume that something is easy or common sense. This can be dangerous if the appropriate amount of training and communication hasn't taken place. Don't make assumptions. Remember, what is common sense to you is not necessarily common sense for someone else. It takes experience, practice, and training for something to become common sense.

11. **Set Goals**—Set goals for yourself and your team that can be achieved in a realistic timeframe. Encourage employees to establish goals with you instead of you setting their goals.

12. **Learn the Value of Balance in Life**— We have talked about this under "Your Legacy." Don't wait until you have lost your family and friends where they won't spend the time of day with you. Don't wait until your health is failing only to realize that you were the one responsible for neglecting and not looking after yourself.

13. **Mistakes**—Mistakes should be forgiven and used as a means of learning. Remove fear where people are afraid to take on initiatives due to the fear of making mistakes. Take responsibility in understanding why the mistake was made and how you can prevent a re-occurrence. In other words, learn from your mistake, so it doesn't happen again.

The Journey – Crossroads to Leadership, Personal and Health and Safety Excellence
Firefighter Crossroad
Do you exhibit some of these traits?

Personal Behavior

You are a high achiever, results-oriented, very organized and a hard worker.

You are internally motivated. You enjoy multitasking.

You are aggressive, sometimes impatient and you set high expectations for others.

You are goal oriented and self driven.

You tend to be reactive instead of proactive.

You often jump to conclusions instead of weighing all the facts.

You finish sentences when people are talking.

You think of a response before a person is finished talking.

You get upset when the car in front of you goes slow (road rage).

You are impatient and will take shortcuts.

You make snap decisions instead of planning and thinking of potential obstacles you may encounter

Leadership Behavior

You are reactive instead of proactive. This could be due to insufficient planning from those above you.

You are aggressive when setting goals and expect others to work as you do.

You often set unrealistic timelines and fail to provide the resources to accomplish the goal without stress.

You tend to make snap decisions without weighing out all your options.

You delegate without taking into consideration the person's present workload.

You are persuasive using a manipulative approach. You sometimes pre-judge.

Communication

You provide both positive and negative feedback during performance appraisals.

You have an open door policy. Your body language shows impatience get to the point behavior.

You fail to give detailed instructions making assumptions the person should know your intensions.

You tend to talk more than listen.

Staff makes assumptions that you are too busy to talk to even if that is not the case.

Health, Safety and Wellness

You are tired and often exhausted due to own pressures and high expectations.

You are prone to headaches and have the potential of having a heart attack or high blood pressure.

You may be subject to anxiety attacks due to your high expectations.

You feel like you have failed if you haven't accomplished what you set out to do.

There is the potential of a high burn out rate, because you push yourself and others beyond the limit.

Your resistance is low causing you to get sick more often.

You are reactive instead of proactive causing rushing and short cuts to fix the problem.

You will often ignore safety procedures to reach the end goal.

You look at immediate first impressions instead of looking for the root cause when there is an incident.

You fail to look at health and safety when attempting to meet production quotas.

FIFTH CROSSROAD

COMMITMENT / RESPONSIBILITY

What will you gain from this chapter?

Embrace the personal and professional rewards when operating at the Commitment/Responsibility Crossroad.
See the positive impact on your life as a whole when you operate at the Commitment/Responsibility Crossroad.
Manage your time as you delegate effectively. Empower your staff.
Set goals where you can leave the other crossroads behind and operate at the Commitment/Responsibility

At each crossroad, we have determined the impact, both personally and as an organization, when we are not committed. I have outlined some points on the following pages. What we encounter personally and as an organization is old news. Sir Winston Churchill says it best: "The price of greatness is responsibility." Fifty years later, we still don't get it. The easy road is no commitment. The more difficult road, with a huge payoff, is commitment. So what gives? How many times do we need to get hit over the head with a two-by-four before we realize the payback of being committed instead of blaming and playing psychological games?

What baggage are you willing to leave behind to reach your true potential
as a person, as a parent, and as a team member within your organization?

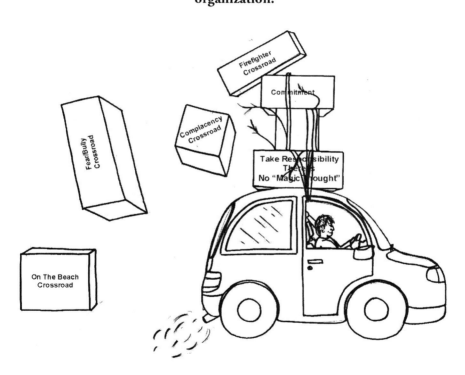

THE COST TO AN ORGANIZATION WHEN THERE IS NO COMMITMENT

➢ The company's vision is not realized because everyone has their own agenda.

➢ The company goes in different directions without sticking to a plan, causing confusion, dissension, and stress.

➢ Morale is low as people operate in phase three and four.

➢ Communication is negative, with blaming, pointing fingers, defensiveness, and rumor mills running rampant.

➢ The environment is built on being reactive instead or proactive.

➢ Labor relations are under a great deal of tension with unionization imminent.

➢ There is high stress, absenteeism, sickness, and a steady flow of talented employees finding another job.

➢ There is low productivity, poor quality, no innovation, and difficulty meeting schedules.

➢ There is a poor financial picture, as there is a loss in market share, a decline in stocks, and an uncertain future.

➢ There is a high potential for accidents.

GREAT BOSS

We have all experienced great bosses and mentors, and quite the opposite, the boss you hate to come to work for.

> <u>Case in Point:</u> *I have been fortunate to have two bosses who stood out from the rest. One you have heard about already. The second was a director for whom I have a great deal of respect and admiration. She always seemed to know when I was out of my comfort zone. She was always there to support and reassure me. I could speak openly to her, voicing my concerns without feeling inadequate.*
>
> *On the flip side, I have also experienced an individual who would scream and use foul language to make his point. This individual worked at the Firefighter Crossroad with little respect for his people, especially if they failed to fulfill his wishes. Our pet expression used to be, "He is having another temper tantrum." Those who knew him would brush it off, and those who did not would be very intimidated and fearful. If he had his way, he would have fired everyone. This was his stress-relief valve.*
>
> *The Firefighter has a difficult time understanding why people do not do the job they have been hired for. As an owner, it makes it difficult to have a successful business when people are operating outside of the Commitment Crossroad. His way of dealing with stress and people not taking responsibility was to have these outbursts.*

Your management team is a critical part to the organization in developing a positive culture where people enjoy coming to work. We probably spend more time with our colleagues than we do with our own family. The success of the organization is based on key decision-makers who can motivate their staff to work toward their vision. This can only be done when everyone is working at the *Commitment Crossroad* where everyone takes responsibility.

Take a moment and think about a boss, colleague, or friend you would do anything for. Write down some of this person's characteristics. Can you see yourself being thought of in the same way?

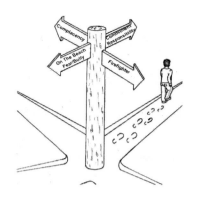

5TH CROSSROAD

COMMITMENT/RESPONSIBILITY

How many of the following points can you truthfully agree you are doing?

How many of these points are you having difficulty with?

Which of these points are you going to commit to, both personally and as an organization?

What is your strategy to implement change within your own personal life and as an organization?

How can you improve health, safety and wellness in your organization 24/7?

MAKING THE TRANSFORMATION TO THE COMMITMENT CROSSROAD

On the Beach

➢ You are where you are, in body and mind.

➢ You are not blaming or being resentful.

➢ You contribute to both your family and your job.

➢ You are taking responsibility for things you can change.

- You are letting go of issues you can't control.
- You are viewing life in a different manner.
- You take responsibility for your health and well-being. You are present in body and mind.
- You take ownership when you fail to follow health and safety procedures, instead of blaming others.

Fear /Bullying

- You have determined your triggers that cause you fear.
- You have realized that to grow, you must step out of your comfort zone.
- You have learned from your past experiences.
- Your communication style is open without a bullying attitude.
- You are making deposits instead of withdrawals.
- You have gotten off of the merry-go-round and eliminated the psychological games.
- You have a legacy to be proud of.
- You have a positive attitude.
- You are unafraid to communicate when you have a safety issue or concern.
- You refrain from being condescending or instilling fear causing people to place their health and well-being at risk.

Complacency

- You are open to new ideas and receptive to change.

➤ You now realize that your complacent attitude not only hinders you as a person, but also everyone around you.

➤ You realize that there are no magic thoughts.

➤ You follow safe operating procedures and refrain from old habits that could cause you injury under different circumstances.

<u>Firefighter</u>

➤ You have realized that you have to slow down.

➤ You respect individuals and realize that everyone is not as internally motivated as you are.

➤ You involve staff more and seek their input before making a decision.

➤ When you delegate, you ensure that the person has the time and skills.

➤ You consider health and safety risks when making decisions.

➤ You discourage shortcuts and rushing when attempting to meet deadlines.

<u>TIPS TO PERSONAL COMMITMENT AND TAKING RESPONSIBILITY</u>
<u>WHAT AREAS CAN YOU IMPROVE ON?</u>

1. **Accepting responsibility**—You accept responsibility instead of shifting the blame.

2. **Leaving your past behind**—You have learned from your past while living in the present. You have let go of problems or concerns that are beyond your control.

3. Mastering fear—You have overcome obstacles that prevent you from moving forward. You have mastered your inner fears in the process.

4. Leaving bullying behind—If you found yourself to be condescending and a bully, you have learned how to communicate and interact without coming across as a bully.

5. Understanding—You are more understanding and are sensitive to people's feelings.

6. Leaving the blame game behind—You refrain from pointing fingers and blaming others.

7. Forgiveness—You have learned the art of forgiveness, both personally and professionally.

8. Encouraging ideas—You encourage ideas from others in both your personal and professional life.

9. Giving credit—You give credit where credit is deserved.

10. Proactive—You are proactive instead of reactive. You assess situations and take time before jumping to a decision that may cost you more stress, money, and aggravation.

11. Calm and stable—You have positive emotions of joy and happiness.

12. Processing data effectively—You see opportunities and welcome ideas from others.

13. Self-actualization—You look at life as a journey of growth and learning.

14. Risk-taker—You are not afraid of trying new challenges.

15. Enthusiastic—You are enthusiastic about the NOW.

16. Commitment to excellence—You are committed to making a difference.

17. Resilient to failure—You look at failure as a means of learning from your mistakes.

18. Balance in life—You have learned how to balance all aspects of your life.

19. Health—You have a healthy lifestyle, including exercise and a balanced diet.

20. Positive relationships—You make a positive impact on people by making them feel good, listening, being encouraging and understanding in both your personal and professional life.

21. High work ethics, integrity, and values—You have good work ethics, integrity, and values.

22. Deposit slips—You make deposits instead of withdrawals.

23. Merry-go-round—You refrain from psychological games and take responsibility for life and your circumstances.

24. Legacy—You have a legacy to be proud of.

25. Continuous learning—You are receptive to continuous learning.

ORGANIZATIONAL EXCELLENCE THROUGH COMMITMENT AND TAKING RESPONSIBILITY,

1) **Vision/mission**—You have shared your vision of where the company is going and laid out a plan on how you will get to your destination.

2) **Employee morale is high as people work in phase two**—Employees are motivated and competent.

3) **Ivory tower approach**—You discourage the ivory tower approach. You make people feel that each and every person within the organization plays an important role to ensure overall success.

4) **Trust, respect for others, and dignity**—Staff members have a high admiration for you as they are treated with trust, respect, and dignity.

5) **Accountability**— As a part of the culture, everyone is held accountable for their performance and health and safety.

6) **Showing presence on the floor**—You manage through observation, being approachable and listening to concerns. You are visible to employees through the means of technology or physically showing your presence.

7) **Positive feedback**—You give positive feedback and acknowledge success when people have mastered an obstacle or when they have gone above and beyond your expectations.

8) **Fair and Consistent**—Employees are treated fairly and consistently throughout the organization.

9) **Learn from your mistakes**—Decision-making is encouraged, allowing people to learn from their mistakes instead of being in fear of termination.

10) **Team player**—You encourage input from other members of the team and give them credit.

11) **Coach and mentor**—You coach and mentor people on an ongoing basis.

12) **Reward**—You reward people with incentives, bonuses, or a simple thank-you.

13) **Continuous learning**—You encourage continuous learning while being open to new ideas.

14) **Empower people**—You empower people instead of controlling them.

15) **Effectively delegate**—You effectively delegate and set the person up for success.

16) **Labor relations are positive**—People enjoy coming to work.

17) **Respect from shareholders**—As an organization, you are respected by shareholders

18) **Rumor mill communication is obsolete**—This occurs when the communication structure is positive and encouraged. There is an exchange of information, which removes the gossip and guessing.

19) **Retention of employees**—Turnover is substantially reduced as people enjoy working.

20) **You are meeting or surpassing productivity and quality standards.**

21) **A methodical problem-solving approach**—This is used to weigh out numerous options.

22) **Health and Safety systems are implemented** to eliminate potential injuries and illnesses both on and off the job. Your safety record shows the fruit of your efforts through zero injuries and illnesses.

23) **The Joint Health and Safety Committee (JHSC) is empowered**— The JHSC recognizes, assesses, and controls hazards with recommendations that are being acted upon.

STEPS TO PROBLEM-SOLVING

Don't Give me a Problem—give me with a solution.

As people, we are burdened with problems on a day-to-day basis, both at work and in our personal life. We have talked throughout on how to overcome various crossroads. I have outlined a problem-solving process that may assist you in identifying and resolving issues you are attempting to work through.

As a manager or supervisor, you sometimes get caught up rescuing people, giving them a solution, or fixing their problems. We are so conditioned to fix the problems of the world; we fail to push the problem back to the person who came up with it in the first place. They want you to look after it instead of taking personal responsibility. If we want the person to grow, they need to think and come up with their own solutions. This makes the person take responsibility and helps them to buy in to the process. This is the best gift you can give a person as a mentor. Support them emotionally and give them time to research and figure out what needs to happen to solve the problem.

As an employee, put your manager's hat on when coming up with solutions. Give your manager some alternatives and the business case on why specific solutions are better than others. Refer to the problem-solving model below to assist you in coming up with solutions to your problems at work as well as at home.

ACTION PLAN—PROBLEM-SOLVING MODEL

➤ **Identify the problem**—What is the problem you are attempting to solve?

➤ **What are the benefits if you solve your problem**—Why solve it?

➤ **Why do you have this problem?**
  o Determine if you or others are operating at a specific crossroad that is causing the problem.
  o Determine if the problem is in or out of your control.
  o Determine the root of the problem and analyze all possibilities.
  o As a manager, determine if it is a non-training or training solution.

➤ **Potential solutions**—Write down numerous solutions to overcome these obstacles. Identify the following:
  o What needs to change in order to pass the obstacle or problem identified?
  o What needs to change to get past a specific crossroad that is giving you grief?
  o Are you willing and ready to make those changes?
  o Do you need outside professional assistance?
  o Are you free to communicate to those who are standing in your way?
  o What is the probability of success with the solution you have identified?
  o What is the business case to support your decision so it can be approved?

- ➢ **Consider the best solution**—Look at all possibilities and assess cost, feasibility, and success rate if you implement the solutions you have decided.
- ➢ **Action plan**—Develop an action plan with specific, achievable, and realistic goals. Determine an appropriate timeframe to complete your action items.
- ➢ **Evaluate and follow up**
  - o Document your actions, especially when meeting legislated requirements.
  - o Evaluate and monitor actions taken to ensure the problem has been eliminated.
  - o Ensure that you have communicated and included people in the process so there is buy-in.
  - o Identify other contributing factors that may be standing in your way.
  - o Modify the plan if the problem has not been rectified.

GOAL-SETTING

Goal-Setting—It is important to look at goal-setting if you want to reach your vision. I think of the elephant. Remember what Howard used to say? "You can't eat the whole elephant, but if you pick one piece at a time, you will see the elephant become manageable." Setting goals is no different. I want to see you REAP rewards as you demolish the whole elephant, reaching the targets you have set out.

R.E.A.P. rewards as you set achievable goals—*Ask yourself the following questions. Is your goal?*

R	**Realistic**
E	**Exact**
A	**Able to be gauged**
P	**Practical with the ability to implement**

1. Realistic—We are setting the person up for failure if we set unrealistic goals. It requires research, problem-solving skills, and the right decision by all parties concerned. Failure to do this will frustrate and de-motivate the employee (or yourself if they are personal goals). You will also lose their respect and trust. Include the person or team members responsible to fulfill your expectations. Work together at determining timeframes and resources

needed. Continue to coach and encourage the team and hold them accountable for the end result.

2. <u>Exact</u>—Your next task is to make the goal exact and not vague. If the goal is too vague, it leaves room for interpretation (e.g., "reduce injuries and illnesses in our workplace" is very general, versus "eliminate injuries and illnesses by 75 percent by 2008." There is NO doubt what your expectations are. From there, you can determine how you are going to eliminate the injuries and illnesses.

3. <u>Able to be gauged</u>—When setting up an action plan to address the elimination of injuries and illnesses 24/7, you need to set realistic timeframes that are achievable. Include people in the process so there is buy-in when it is time to implement your plan. Designate specific responsibility for completion of objectives, as well as what happens if objectives are not met. By doing this, you can gauge whether you were overzealous or whether the team's commitment was lacking. This allows you to revisit the project and determine what needs to be done to get back on track. This also provides a tool to be used at performance appraisal time. If you are looking at your own personal goals, do the same. If you don't set goals, there is nothing to work toward.

4. <u>Practical with the ability to implement</u>—This is the part where you have to remember to not attempt to eat the whole elephant. If you bite piece by piece, setting timelines, it becomes practical and easy to implement without

overwhelming yourself or others. It is difficult to expect someone to achieve a goal if they don't see the light at the end of the tunnel. Again, if we get the individual's buy-in, then there are no surprises if the goal isn't achieved. It now becomes a performance issue.

a. Ensure that the person has the skills, knowledge, resources, and time to complete the task.

b. Consider the person's workload, and include the person in the process.

c. Get buy-in from the person being assigned the project or task.

d. Mutually agree on the goal to be achieved.

e. Most of all support the person emotionally to help remove inner fears. If they have difficulty with roadblocks that may be in their way. Do not rescue them until the person has exhausted all potential solutions.

f. Lastly, praise (and in some cases, depending on the complexity of the goal) and reward the person. Let them know you appreciate their endeavors. This includes giving yourself a reward when you have achieved your own personal goals.

COMMITMENT

TAKING 100% RESPONSIBILITY
PERSONALLY AND PROFESSIONALLY

1. What crossroads are you have difficulty passing?

2. What are the obstacles that are preventing you from moving on?

3. What obstacles are within your control?

4. What obstacles are out of your control? Can you dismiss them and move on?

5. What are you willing to do in order to move past these obstacles?

6. Would you be happier if you were committed and overcame these obstacles?

7. What would your personal and professional life look like if you addressed some of these obstacles and moved into the *Commitment/Taking Responsibility Crossroad?*

8. What positive impact would you have on the people around you?

9. What areas can you improve on to continue being safe and healthy 24/7?

The Journey – Crossroads to Leadership, Personal and Health and Safety Excellence
Commitment Crossroad
Do you exhibit some of these traits?

Personal Behavior

You are competent, trained, skilled, capable and proficient.

You accept responsibility, you are organized, flexible and adaptable

You are open minded, honest, loyal, building trust with people and you do not compromise your integrity

You respect people and their differences. You listen as well as being forgiving without wanting to take revenge.

You lead by example both at home and at work keeping your promises.

You are proactive instead of reactive taking time to implement plans with the assistance of team members

You are committed to excellence with positive emotions. You are enthusiastic and encourage ideas

You are customer service oriented who exhibits excellent people skills.

You encourage continuously learning as you are forward thinking and able to think outside of the box.

Leadership Behavior

You often walk around the area you are managing making yourself approachable.

You encourage participation. People are valued and appreciated.

People know what is expected of them. You have a down-to-earth approach.

You are an excellent coach and mentor. You praise employees for a job well done

A team approach is fostered as you are involved with your staff encouraging ideas.

You are a true leader where people respect, trust and are loyal to you.

You are viewed as fair, a good listener and sensitive to people's frustrations.

You empower and encourage staff to reach their full potential. You allow for mistakes with the goal of learning from them.

You are results-oriented. You have values that you live by and you respect cultural diversity.

You foster an environment where fear and bullying is eliminated through positive communication.

You do not tolerate bullying from employees or peers.

Communication

You have excellent communication skills and encourage participation.
You are an effective listener. You keep people informed as well as
including them in goal-setting and project planning.

You give candid feedback on appraisals with the intent to learn and grow.
You keep people informed. You are approachable. You are positive when
thinking and speaking. You discourage a negative environment.

You communicate health and safety expectations. You have a good
working relationship with staff.

You remove fear by using appropriate body language and tone of voice.

Health, Safety and Wellness

Commitment comes from the top with the senior management team supporting health and safety.

You have a "positive health and safety culture" where everyone takes responsibility for health and safety.

You have a continuous improvement plan with policies and procedures that have been communicated effectively.

Your staff is properly trained and evaluated ensuring they understand your expectations.

Safety is included in all aspects of the business. Safety is measured and included in performance appraisals.

Silence = Permission is not supported. There are consequences for health and safety infractions.

Employees take safety seriously and watch out for one another.

You are proactive instead of reactive. Recommendations are acted upon.

JHSC is fully supported with ideas being valued.

Thorough accident investigations are conducted analyzing to find out the root cause of why it happened with corrective action implemented.

Part II

FIRST TOOL

VISION

What will you gain from this chapter?

Vision does not only apply to an organization; it applies to our life as a whole and to our health and well-being.

Understand the importance of creating your personal vision of where you want to be in life.

Understand the importance of an organization having a clear vision of eliminating injuries and illnesses 24/7.

Recognize that your health and safety policy is not just something posted in the front lobby, but something that you truly believe in.

Understand as a leader, it is your job to engage your people to see your vision and climb aboard.

YOUR PERSONAL VISION—What do you personally want in your life? If you are operating at the *Commitment Crossroad*, you have worked through many of your obstacles and set goals. Visualize your aspirations and follow them up with positive affirmation statements. You want to focus on "I can do" even if at the moment you are not sure how it is going to happen.

Case in Point: *Many motivational speakers talk about visualization. It is suggested that you put a*

picture of what you want where you can readily
see it. e.g. a new house or a new car. This acts as
a reminder of what your end goal is. How are you
going to buy that new car or new house? Have
you mapped out a plan? Visualize what you want
or where you want to be. Think positive without
letting negative thoughts cloud your vision.

<u>YOUR VISION</u>—As a leader, your job is to share your vision, values and beliefs with the people who can help make it happen. Your excitement will be their inspiration. As their leader, it is your responsibility to set the course and lead them towards the end goal.

<u>COMMON TRAITS OF THE IDEAL LEADER</u>

- ➤ You are honest, credible and you have integrity standing up for your code of ethics.
- ➤ You are clear about your values and beliefs.
- ➤ You function at the *Commitment Crossroad* being committed to the end goal.
- ➤ You Lead by Example.
- ➤ You inspire people through effective communication, coaching and mentoring.
- ➤ You build trust through caring, being fair, respectful and taking responsibility.
- ➤ You provide the tools and resources to your people while removing potential obstacles that may prevent them from achieving the goals you have set out.
- ➤ You have included in your vision your desire to eliminate injuries and illnesses both on and off the job.

REALIZING YOUR VISION—To realize your vision you will want to ensure you have certain aspects in place:

> You share your vision getting employees buy-in.
> You ensure people have the skills and knowledge to anticipate roadblocks and accomplish objectives you have laid out in a realistic timeframe.
> You know your market and how you intend to succeed.
> You include in the plan a "What's in it for me?" philosophy so employees will be excited to be part of the team.
> You have the resources available to execute your plan. This includes a budget for people, materials, equipment and processes required to make the organization a success.

MANAGER OR SUPERVISOR—The manager or supervisor is the driving force in seeing the vision realized. They must exhibit the same traits as a leader while motivating, coaching, mentoring, and inspiring employees under them to be excited about the journey ahead.

HEALTH AND SAFETY—VISION

As much as you need a vision to set the course for the organization, you also need a vision for health and safety. Your commitment and belief that injuries and illnesses both on and off the job can be eliminated is critical when implementing your health and safety system. Without your true commitment, your health and safety system will struggle. Companies benefit time and time again when they make health and safety a priority and a part of doing business.

Your starting point in communicating your commitment is to develop a written health and safety policy that is not just words, but what you truly believe in and support. It needs to capture the importance that it is everyone's responsibility to prevent accidents and injuries. See Part III on tips in developing a positive health and safety culture.

SECOND TOOL

MISSION AND VALUES

What will you gain from this chapter?

Recognize the importance of having a mission or
means of getting to your destination.
Recognize the importance of having personal and
organizational values to live by.
Establish a means of executing how you are going to get to your destination.
Address the role your people will play as you implement your plan.
Understand the importance of outlining your values
as an organization and adhering to them.

YOUR PERSONAL MISSION AND VALUES—We think of "mission" and "values" in business, but do we consider what our mission and values are in our personal life? You have established your vision in the previous chapter. Your next step is figuring out how you are going to get to your destination. This is set out through your mission or setting goals. Remember to make these goals small and achievable. This eliminates frustration and giving up. It is important to identify and not compromise your values, even when temptation knocks at your door. How many movie stars or prominent people do we read about whose past decisions have come back to haunt them? Don't have regrets because you compromised your values

<u>MISSION IN AN ORGANIZATION</u> — As an organization, determining your mission is senior management's task. Once you have established your mission, your next step is to get your people on board. Your excitement is contagious as you include your people. Think of a group of people who are excited about a cause. They come together in the most difficult times and support the cause. The same applies in business. People need a sense of purpose and belonging. They need to feel appreciated and know that their input is valued. When morale is high and everyone is working together, everything falls into place.

Part of your strategy is to include "What's in it for me?" This may include incentives or perks when established goals have been accomplished. This shows your appreciation and proves your commitment to not only the organization but to the people who were responsible for getting you to your destination. Think how people feel when they have done their very best, gone above and beyond your expectations—and then get nothing in return. They see the company's profits go up, they see the executives getting bonuses, but the people who made it happen get nothing. There goes your morale down the drain. Don't be greedy; share the wealth and more will come.

<u>VALUES IN AN ORGANIZATION</u> describes the acceptable behaviors that will get you to your destination. You need to look at the following when establishing your values. Your values are specific behaviors that are determined by everyone involved. Without buy-in from all concerned, it is difficult to operate at the *Commitment Crossroad*. This may include respect, integrity, honesty, quality, excellent customer service and the list goes on. Predetermined values give you a code of conduct to work by. It is a reminder to not compromise our integrity to reach our vision.

Your values need to be widely communicated and agreed upon. People need to understand the importance of adhering to your values to maintain the integrity of the company. It is important to communicate that if your values are not practiced, there will be consequences. On the flip side, people need to be praised and rewarded when values are practiced and when people achieve goals that help the organization realize their vision. Your values should include caring for and valuing your people. This includes a systematic approach in developing a positive health and safety culture where injuries and illnesses are unacceptable, both on and off the job.

HEALTH AND SAFETY
MISSION—VALUES

I think we can agree that when we walk out our front door, we intend to come back the same way, with no injuries or illnesses. That seems like common sense, and yet people are injured or killed on a daily basis.

Include health and safety into the organization's vision, mission, and values, to ensure that this facet of the business is not compromised. Promote the idea of creating a positive health and safety culture 24/7, both on and off the job. Find the "hook" where people are willing to take responsibility for their health, safety and wellbeing. Strategize a plan where people realize the physical and emotional consequences of *"The Magic Thought – Can't Happen to Me."* Help people realize that their actions or inactions could alter their life forever.

This starts with your health and safety policy, which outlines your commitment and the commitment of everyone within the organization. My philosophy also includes the importance of off-the-job safety. You are endeavoring to create a habit where people think about their health, safety, and their well-being all of the time. This may require additional budget as you set up information sessions, newsletters, and other means to bring safety home to family and friends.

Your mission should include the philosophy that injuries and illnesses are preventable when everyone takes responsibility and is committed. Included in this mission is that people at all levels of the organization, leave their excessive baggage at each crossroad, with the goal that everyone is working at the *Commitment Crossroad*"

Part of your mission is to implement health and safety systems that are included into your existing management systems. There is a step-by-step process to follow in Part III when developing your health and safety system to support your vision.

Values are essential when eliminating injuries and illnesses. Is the organization willing to compromise everyone's health and well-being to meet production deadlines or to compete in this global marketplace? This becomes difficult as you balance the pendulum. Your profit margins are tight, you want quality at a fair price, and most importantly, you want everyone to be injury-free. The part you need to get your head around is the cost if someone is injured. There goes your profit. We will address the benefits of an effective health and safety system later in this book, but in the meantime, consider including your values for health and safety in your code of conduct. A few examples include working safely without performing unsafe practices; cleaning as you go so slip and trip hazards are removed; no horseplay, or communicating when you observe unsafe conditions or practices.

THIRD TOOL

COMMUNICATION

What will you gain from this chapter?

Understand the importance of effective communication.
See how your body language and tone of voice can affect your message.
Understand how your communication skills can cause Fear
See how you may be perceived as a bully because of your actions.
Realize how loosely we use the phrase common sense.

EFFECTIVE COMMUNICATION

Body language, effective listening, what you say, how you say it, and your tone of voice reflects whether the communication has a positive or negative impact.

> ➤ **Body language can send out many messages, both positive and negative.**
>   - o   Maintain eye contact when having a conversation with someone.
>   - o   Use affirmative head nods and paraphrase to show you are listening and interested.
>   - o   Facial expressions are a dead giveaway that you are interested, angry, or bored.

o Folding your arms will convey that you are angry or impatient.

o Do not interrupt the speaker. Give them your attention and respect what they have to say.

➤ **Be conscious of tone**—Your tone of voice can send negative messages to the person listening. Although you are frustrated or having a bad day, be cautious of how you are coming across as you verbalize your thoughts. Your tone of voice can affect how the information is received.

➤ **Be sensitive and empathetic to people's feelings**—Be sensitive to people's feelings and cultural differences.

➤ **Buy in on an idea**—Have the person reiterate what you have said, to ensure they have understood and agree with you. Provide a safe environment where people can advise of their concerns or differences. Their participation is critical in getting their buy-in. They can offer some valuable ideas, feel like they belong and are part of the process. It also is a great motivator and retention booster. People feel valued and excited as their ideas are considered and implemented.

➤ **When e-mailing**—When writing an e-mail, don't shout at the person by using all caps, highlighting, or using a different color. Tone can be identified depending on how you write. Often we hammer out a message and press SEND, not realizing that our frustration or anger is showing in the way we have written. If you are writing out of frustration or anger, save it and revisit it later before sending. This gives you an opportunity to rephrase the thought in order to eliminate the tone you may have exhibited when writing the message initially.

BARRIERS IN COMMUNICATION

There may be barriers, which can prevent the message from being received and understood. We can look at various crossroads that hinder the communication process.

> ➤ <u>On the Beach</u> —"Here in body, but not in mind." The person is not interested. They have tuned you out as they are thinking of something else.

> ➤ <u>Fear /Bullying</u>—Fear of being disciplined or speaking up. The *Bully* is condescending and uses inappropriate body language and tone to make his or her point. People are afraid to voice their concerns or ideas when fear and/ or bullying are present. People feel their environment is unsafe to work in because nothing is done to correct health and safety deficiencies. The perception is to keep your mouth shut and do your work. This crossroad is a must to get past, if communication lines are to be positive and open.

> ➤ <u>Complacent</u>—This person is closed-minded and happy the way things are. They have always done a task a certain way with *The Magic Thought – Can't Happen to Me* view.

They are resistant to change, which makes effective communication a challenge.

➢ Firefighter—There is no time to communicate, as this person is in a crisis mode. These people are rushed, hurried, and sometimes jump to conclusions. Their body language is usually a dead giveaway: "Hurry up and let me get on with what I was doing." This is where the firefighter needs to take a step back and let people voice their opinions, concerns, and ideas without being impatient.

➢ Commitment— Barriers have been removed as everyone is committed. People operating at the *Commitment Crossroad,* listen and use appropriate body language to show they have heard what you have to say. People will open up freely knowing that the person they are talking to are interested, have respect and understand what has been said. Obstacles from previous crossroads have been removed.

TIPS TO OVERCOME SOME OF THESE BARRIERS:

1. Communicate at the *Commitment Crossroad.*
2. Listen without pre-judging or getting angry, while creating a non-threatening environment.
3. Ask questions or paraphrase to better understand and clarify points that are unclear.
4. Use positive body language and watch your tone of voice so your intentions are not misinterpreted.

5. Look at the most effective way to communicate a thought (e.g., face-to-face, written, e-mail, etc.).

6. Help the person see the benefit in what you are suggesting while including them in the process.

7. Keep lines of communication open to keep people informed.

8. End your conversation on a positive note to ensure that they understand the intent of the conversation.

9. Stay focused and be patient. Be open-minded and focus on the issue, not the personality.

10. Listen without interrupting. Respect each other's views.

STEPS IN MANAGING CONFLICT

1. Enter a conversation with an open mind without pre-judging.

2. Use appropriate body language and tone. If you are aggressive with an elevated voice or exhibit tone, chances are, the person you are communicating with will exhibit the same behavior unless he/she knows better. If they are screaming, use a monotone, even tone of voice. This makes the person stop and listen.

3. Ask for help to understand their point of view or frustration.

4. Exercise patience, as people handle frustrations differently.

5. Before coming to a conclusion, gather all the facts, be sympathetic and understanding as to where the person is coming from. Sometimes we look at a situation as being common sense or not a big deal. Meanwhile the person experiencing the situation is having great difficulty with it. This may be caused by past experiences, perceptions or something that is going on in their personal life. Your job is to listen and develop an understanding to enable you to defuse the situation.

6. Most important, LISTEN to each other. Don't pre-judge and think you are the only one who could be right. Talk about each other's frustrations using appropriate communication skills, remove any barriers or bias, and objectively look at the problem.

7. Mutually work together to come up with a solution to the problem.

8. Take responsibility in correcting the problem without blaming, accusing or becoming defensive.

9. After looking at each other's views, determine a plan of action to overcome the conflict.

COMMUNICATION AT THE COMMITMENT CROSSROAD

Communicating effectively builds trust, respect, and most of all, breaks down barriers as we seek to understand one another.

You have overcome obstacles at the previous crossroads to enable you to operate at this crossroad.

> You are open to suggestions and ideas while respecting each other's differences.
> You don't jump to conclusions. Instead, you seek to understand without judging.
> You are aware of your body language and tone, ensuring that you are sending the right message.
> You allow the person to communicate their views without interrupting and without formulating an answer before the person has finished.
> You listen and try to understand where the other person is coming from.
> You do not bully or intimidate people.
> You are not condescending.
> You don't become defensive when someone comes to you with a situation.

CREATE A POSITIVE HEALTH AND SAFETY CULTURE
COMMUNICATING HEALTH AND SAFETY AT THE COMMITMENT CROSSROAD

Effective communication when handling health and safety issues is imperative to eliminate accidents and injuries. Perception of being terminated, fear of repercussions, or concerns about what people think prevent the reporting of unsafe conditions or the voicing of concerns. Past experiences and circumstances contribute to these perceptions.

As a member of the management team, your challenge is to get people to realize the importance of reporting safety concerns and not taking chances with their health and well-being. You want to instill the importance of reporting hazards without reprisal. Communicate that there are no stupid questions.

> Reaffirm that you appreciate their concerns and value their input.

> Create a positive health and safety culture, removing fear.

> Communicate during orientation or pre-operational meetings the importance of voicing health and safety concerns and asking questions.

> Implement a hazard-reporting procedure so people know how to report unsafe conditions or practices.

> Communicate health and safety policies and procedures.

> There should be no reprisals when someone refuses or asks questions that involve their health and safety. (This is against the law in Ontario, Canada)

> Act on recommendations when brought to your attention and follow through on promises.

> Support your Joint Health and Safety Committee by giving them time to perform their duties, appropriate training as well as addressing their recommendations.

> Ensure that people are competent to perform the task assigned. Train people on expectations or operations. Allow time for practical application. Continue to observe and retrain if there is confusion. DO NOT ASSUME that a person should know something because you did the classroom training. Pair the person up with another co-worker, continue to coach and observe, ensuring that the person understands the task they are performing. When we have done something for a period of time, it becomes "common sense." Remember, what is common sense to you is not automatically common sense to someone else.

COMMON SENSE, YOU SAY?

As mentioned earlier under "The Purpose of this Book," I wrote an article on "Common Sense, You Say? Outlined below is the article that was published in the local newspaper. See what my perception is, when it comes to common sense.

I didn't realize how loosely we use the words "common sense" as we are talking to people. It wasn't until a colleague I have known for a number of years suggested that I write about common sense. This was back in the summer, and at the time, I dismissed it from my mind. Funny enough, the words "common sense" kept on popping up. Well, here I am and our topic of the day is none other than "common sense." First, let's be clear on the true meaning: Common means "shared together" and sense means, "to grasp or comprehend." Together, they spell "common sense." Using a simple analogy, if you were brought up in a jungle, it may not be common sense that a switch on the side of a wall will give you light. So you see, what is common to one is not common to all. Our experiences, training, and knowledge will help dictate whether something is "common sense."

We ASSUME—whoops, we know what happens when we assume—that an individual should know what we are asking. You send an employee on what seems to be a simple task only to find that they had no idea what you wanted. You're giving a computer-training course, assuming that everyone will know how to turn the computer on and find the program you want him or her to work on. You see it as "common sense." Not! We too often assume that what is commonplace for us should be commonplace for someone else. The difference is that someone else may never have been exposed to that particular experience. When you ask someone to do something, think of their mind as being a clean slate that knows nothing. Your job is to fill the mind with what you want or what your expectations are. I am sure we all have been in a situation where an employee is not meeting the standards we have set. Before criticizing them, step back and take a hard look. Did you do everything in your power to train, coach and share your expectations with them? Don't assume they should know something if you haven't taken the time to be specific.

I look at a business operation, and things I see as "common sense" to be successful are: encouraging employee participation, setting goals and a vision of where you want to be and sharing them with your employees, involving your employees in setting objectives, treating people the way you would want to be treated, caring and listening, being approachable so employees are not afraid to tell you if they made a mistake. For me, this is "common sense." How could you operate a business any other way? I have come to this conclusion because of past experiences where employees got feedback only when they did something wrong. They were terminated without a progressive discipline approach to correct the undesired behavior. Their toxic workplace included yelling and profanity all part of the Fear /Bullying Crossroad. On the flip side, I have worked for organizations that cared, provided fabulous coaching and development, encouraged their employees to participate, and coached employees to step out of their comfort zone. I have been able to look at both sides and without a doubt have seen the advantage of operating at the Commitment Crossroad and valuing your most important commodity—your people.

For the person who has only been in an environment of negativity with a lack of participation, goal-setting, coaching, and mentoring, you look at me and ask, "How can you say, "that's common sense?"" You see, my values and beliefs have been molded by my past experiences, knowledge, and are part of who I am. I have internalized what I believe works, so for me, it is "common sense."

The point I am making is that before you say the words "That's common sense," sit back and evaluate the situation. Through your own experiences, your perception is that it is "common sense" and everyone should know. Share your knowledge and experience so that we can each comprehend what is expected of us, therefore establishing "common sense" among all of us. Once we have properly coached, trained, shared our expectations, people will be able to look through your eyes, and say "That's common sense." Follow through with this whether it is employee relations, health and safety, business planning, customer service, or sales and marketing. Never assume what you perceive as being "common sense."

FOURTH TOOL

VOICE, DIGNITY, RESPECT, TRUST, INTEGRITY, HONESTY, LOYALTY

What will you gain from this chapter?

Motivate people by listening and giving them an opportunity
to voice their concerns or offer valuable input.
Recognize the importance of giving people dignity and respect.
See the respect among your colleagues when you
display integrity, honesty, and loyalty.

Quotations

Every person wants "voice" and "dignity."—Jack Welch[4]
People want dignity and respect. Tom Peters—*In Search of Excellence*

IMPACT ON OUR LIFE WHEN WE DON'T LIVE BY OUR VALUES—You will struggle to be successful in any part of your life if you have not included voice, dignity, respect, trust, integrity, honesty, and loyalty as part of your values and your internal being. You may be wealthy in terms of money, but if you have compromised the above to get there, was it worth it? Are you truly happy when you have walked over others to get what you

---

wanted? Remember, we discussed earlier: "What is your legacy?" Money and fame aren't everything.

VOICE

I think in many cases we concentrate on what we have to say, instead of encouraging others to contribute to a conversation or a problem at hand. We fail to listen and encourage ideas.

AT HOME we have lost the family connection around the dinner table. Instead everyone goes their separate ways as we focus on television or are too busy to make the time for each other. There isn't the same kind of closeness due to our hectic environments. We have become materialistic, constantly striving for more leaving no time to foster communication or voice. In many cases, Mom and Dad work just to keep a roof over their heads. As our new generation has acquired their university degree to get ahead in life, they must continue working to maintain their status and pay off the hefty loans they have acquired. As we juggle our work and home lives, there is no quality time to communicate and build a solid foundation of trust and respect with our kids. We tend to judge and voice our opinions instead of allowing our children to speak and voice their concerns without being a bully. We then wonder why our kids don't tell us about what is going on.

> Case in Point: *My husband and I spent endless hours with our kids building trust, giving them values and opening the communication door so they could talk freely without fear of consequences. We laid the foundation the best that we could at the beginning. We enjoyed many vacations, went for numerous walks with the dogs and always had*

dinner together in the kitchen not in front of the television. They shared their frustrations, fears and joys with us as we shared quality time together. We gave them "voice" where they would not get in trouble if they confided in us.

Trust doesn't just happen. It takes years of an encouraging *Voice* and listening to develop the trust and respect that is needed, as your kids get older. Our job is to build values and let them know that we are there for them unconditionally.

<u>AT WORK</u>—Trust is equally important. I hope that as a manager, you are operating at the *Commitment Crossroad*. If this is the case, you are giving *Voice* to your employees. You have empowered your employees and have encouraged a participative environment where you encourage and value their ideas. You involve employees in the decision-making and implementation processes. You act on employee concerns, no matter how trivial. You listen without interrupting. You respect what they have to say. You encourage employees to look at a solution instead of giving you the problem. You allow for mistakes, mentor and coach with the goal of learning from your mistakes.

<u>Case in Point</u>: *I have encountered many occasions where employees had ideas about making a task easier or more affordable. Because they were not encouraged to voice their opinion, they sat back and watched in silence, only to advise later that there was an easier way. This is a good example of how people end up On the Beach or in "Phase Three," as mentioned before.*

As Jack Welch notes in his book Winning, "You paid me for my hands when you could have had my brains as well—for nothing."[5]

[5] *Winning* by Jack Welch with Suzy Welch – p. 56

DIGNITY AND RESPECT

Respect is earned by what you say and do. When you compromise someone's dignity, you are compromising his or her respect for you. Once you lose someone's respect, it is difficult to get it back.

AT HOME—This not only applies at work, but also at home with the people we love. We sometimes get frustrated with our children or our elderly parents. We live in such a fast-paced environment that we get impatient and become self-centered. We don't think about how they feel. We want to be right, so we fail to listen to sage advice from the elderly, forgetting that they were once where we are. We may not agree with our parents' values, beliefs, or opinions, but we should at least respect them. We fail to take time with our kids or to listen to and respect their views. Often their dignity is compromised as the parent openly screams at them in front of other people when the child exhibits an undesired behavior.

> Case in Point: *Look at our hockey arenas. Unless it has changed, it is common for parents to scream and criticize the kids on the ice. If a player makes a bad play, the parents are on his or her case right away. They want the win at all cost. They fail to realize the message that is being sent when they scream and use abusive language in front of other people. How demoralizing is it when you attack their dignity in front of their colleagues and with people watching?* They made a mistake. *Do we forget they are kids?*

AT WORK—I often think that people don't even realize how their actions, body language, and verbal abuse can affect someone's dignity. It can also show a lack of respect. You may not approve of someone's values or beliefs, but at least give them the respect and dignity they deserve.

For those who operate at the *Bullying Crossroad*, it is a normal practice to instill fear and judge people. Your attitude—consisting of being condescending, making people feel inadequate, judging them, or making smart jokes—contributes to a lack of respect. Your behavior does not allow the person to have dignity. You want to be in control at the expense of other people. You do not care or respect the feelings of others. Put the shoe on the other foot when you operate at this crossroad. How would you feel in the same situation if the circumstances were reversed?

We also forget that we are all different. We process information at a different pace and in a different way. Some of us are visual learners, where others prefer information in writing. Some need to be shown and then need to actually do it themselves before they grasp the concept. This requires patience, respect, and giving the person dignity so they don't feel stupid. It is easy for you, because you have internalized and know what you are trying to explain. This is not the case for the new person who is attempting to understand a concept or your expectations for the first time.

> Case in Point: *A co-op student was helping one summer. She was busy completing a trend analysis on my computer that we shared. We also needed to get some photocopying done for an upcoming seminar. I told her to continue what she was doing and I would do the photocopying. She couldn't believe that her boss was going to do her job while she finished. My mindset was that two jobs needed to get done. I thought nothing of pitching in. The*

respect I gained was huge. It seemed common sense
and normal. Work together as a team.

<u>Case in Point:</u> *There was a supervisor for whom my*
husband had the greatest admiration and respect.
He would play hockey with the old-timers and made
it clear that work stayed at work. He was one of
the guys at this point. When he walked through the
gate, his employees knew exactly where they stood. If
they messed up, they would hear about it, but by the
same token, he would listen to his employees and be
there for them. People knew where they stood with
him and respected the fact that he had a job to do
without favouritism or being afraid of what people
would say. People went out of their way to do a good
job because of the respect, trust, and loyalty he had
fostered.

TRUST

Building trust takes time and must be earned no differently than respect. You need integrity, honesty, and loyalty if you are going to develop trust.

<u>AT HOME</u>—Building trust is a necessity in whatever relationship you have. If you look at the number of marriages that break up due to the lack of trust and being honest, it is mind-boggling. When we look at raising our children, we hope we have set the foundation for them to make wise decisions. You need to know when you can trust your kids and when they still need your guidance. Kids and family members need to realize that if they want your trust and respect, they need to be honest. As a parent, when we say we are going to do something, we need to follow through; otherwise, trust is being compromised.

AT WORK—In business, trust is vitally important, because without trust, you have the grapevine of canteen lawyers coming up with their own perceptions of what is going on. Without trust, there is no voice. People won't communicate, because they don't trust what you will do with the information. Keeping people in the loop on what is happening, how they will be impacted, and what your intentions are is very important. If you commit to doing something, then follow through with it. Keep your promises. You are far better to evaluate your time and schedule before committing and saying yes. By the same token, if someone comes to you with an issue address it and get back to the individual with an answer; otherwise, there is no point in coming to you. The perception is then, "You won't do anything, so why bother?" Learn to say no when you are unable to commit. Effective listening without judgment is another way of building trust with people. When someone communicates something that is confidential, you respect him or her by keeping it confidential. If it is necessary to share the information with a person, explain the reason why you must share the information so the individual understands.

INTEGRITY

Integrity is part of who you are. Your values and beliefs are tied closely to your integrity. What are you willing to compromise? What regrets will you have in the future for the decision you have made? Your integrity says a lot about your values. Someone who is dishonest or lies compromises his or her integrity. By the same token, you lose trust because people are unwilling to believe what you are saying or what you have promised to do. One of the reasons for establishing values in an organization is to help maintain integrity. It gives people a code of conduct on acceptable practices. A person knows their boundaries. They know what is acceptable and what is not acceptable.

HONESTY

Are you willing to sacrifice your integrity and trust with people due to dishonesty? There are various reasons why people refrain from being honest. Typically we don't want to hurt someone's feelings, we fear consequences, we fear being judged, or we fear what people are going to think. There is also dishonesty when people either steal time or material things. Dishonesty is probably the one area that can get you into the most trouble. Depending on the situation, your worse case scenario is that you are terminated or criminally charged for stealing. As a person, you are no longer creditable, you cannot be trusted and you have lost respect. Trust and respect is extremely important when working with people. It is something that is earned. It just doesn't happen on its own. It is also something difficult to get back.

AT HOME—Are you honest with family members or do you keep your frustrations inside, never letting them know how you feel? Have you created a safe environment where there is trust and respect? Honesty is a value that is instilled from the beginning. You need to remove obstacles and create an open door where you are trusted and are willing to listen without judgment.

Case in Point: *How many people walk away*
from relationships because they cannot be honest

with each other? I can say, from a personal aspect, being married for a long period of time has been hard work, but well worth it. There have been times where we were faced with obstacles but overcame them. Open communication, honesty, understanding, patience, and unconditional love have brought us closer than ever. Don't throw the towel in until you have been honest with each other and taken personal responsibility for what is not working. It takes two to tango.

AT WORK—Are you honest with people when they are not meeting performance expectations? People need to know the repercussions if they are dishonest with you. If you want to build trust and respect with your colleagues, then be honest. My favorite expression during orientation was, "I can handle a mistake. What I can't handle is covering up or not admitting to a mistake. Be upfront and we can deal with it; otherwise, depending on the situation, it may cost you your job."

Case in Point: *During training sessions, I made it quite clear that if employees ran into a problem, they were to notify their supervisor immediately. They were also advised that their job could be on the line if they failed to communicate important issues where the company could be at risk. I also said that mistakes happen and we learn from them, but if mistakes are made and you are dishonest or hold back, there is an integrity issue at stake—not to mention a liability issue for the company, depending on the situation. People knew our expectations as an organization as well as the consequences if they failed to follow through on those expectations.*

There was a situation where a major highway was shut down due to a spill. The driver called his supervisor to tell him he was stuck alongside of the

*road, but said nothing about the spill. We received
a call from an outsider. This individual was a good
driver, good with customers, but he made a fatal
mistake that cost him his job due to his dishonesty.
The company won the wrongful dismissal suit due
to the thorough training and communication we
had done. There was no question what the driver's
responsibility was. If he were honest, we would
have dealt with it differently. We made it very
clear the importance of reporting situations to their
supervisor. He shut down a major highway and
withheld information. This error cost him his job.*

VOICE, DIGNITY, RESPECT, TRUST, INTEGRITY, HONESTY, LOYALTY
Some ways to foster voice, dignity, respect, trust, integrity, honesty and loyalty.

1. Operate at the *Commitment Crossroad*, where all other crossroads have been surpassed.
2. Include the importance of voice, dignity, respect, trust, integrity, honesty, and loyalty in your values.
3. Use effective communication skills listening to people's frustrations and coaching them.
4. Make time for people at home and at work.
5. Empower people by including them in the process.
6. Allow for mistakes that people can learn from.
7. Create a safe environment where people will come forward, leaving behind their false perceptions.
8. Acknowledge people and speak to them as you see them.
9. Realize that each and every one of us plays an important role in the organization's success.

10. Encourage an open-door policy where people see you as being approachable.
11. Encourage that there are no stupid questions or concerns.
12. Be visible.
13. Respect people's opinions and their differences. Don't pre-judge.
14. Keep information confidential unless you predetermine that the information should be shared.
15. Be fair and objective letting people know the consequences when expectations are not met.
16. Encourage and praise people, helping them get past their fear. I would share stories of my own fear. This helped them understand that we all have fear but we learn to overcome and move ahead to grow.
17. Say "thank you." This includes when managing your home life. Don't take for granted the little extras that people do for you.
18. Be sensitive and understanding. Often I was accused of "mothering" my employees. If that is a criticism on my management style, I take it as a compliment. How many people are fortunate to have someone, including his or her parents, caring about them?
19. Keep your promises. Plan and determine your time and resources before committing.
20. Once you commit to something, follow through, don't procrastinate or back out.
21. Recognize and respect diversity, gender, and age. We are all here for the same purpose.
22. Use a down-to-earth approach, recognizing that each and every one of us has a significant purpose to ensure the

success of an organization. Never have the attitude, "it's beneath me."

BENEFITS OF VOICE, DIGNITY, RESPECT, TRUST, INTEGRITY, HONESTY, AND LOYALTY

➤ Your people will operate at the *Commitment Crossroad* in phase two, being motivated and competent.

➤ People will be excited to come to work, as they feel they are making a difference.

➤ You empower people by listening and encouraging input.

➤ You build trust by keeping promises. You show you care.

➤ People know where you stand when you don't compromise your integrity.

➤ You increase productivity and morale as people learn to trust and respect you.

➤ You give people a sense of self-worth as you respect their differences.

➤ You work as a team at work and at home, understanding each other's views and differences.

➤ Honesty makes people accountable. It forces them to take responsibility for their actions.

➤ You eliminate the "grapevine" or "water cooler" effect by being open and honest.

➤ When you respect, build trust, and are honest with people, their commitment to meet your expectations is far greater.

➤ You build a legacy where you are respected, trusted, and remembered.

CREATE A POSITIVE HEALTH AND SAFETY CULTURE
VOICE, DIGNITY, RESPECT, TRUST, INTEGRITY, HONESTY, AND LOYALTY

Voice, dignity, respect, trust, integrity, and honesty play an important part in health and safety. These areas can either make or break your Internal Responsibility System.

➤ VOICE – Encouraging people to report hazards or areas of concern is critical in preventing accidents or incidents. This can only happen if you exhibit excellent communication skills, and effective listening with an attitude that there are no stupid questions. Remember, it may seem common sense to you but not to them, so patience and making someone feel comfortable are key to encouraging voice. Your job is to remove fear, so people will come forward, voicing their concerns. Your Joint Health and Safety Committee can play a key role in building a positive atmosphere where communication is encouraged.

➤ DIGNITY AND RESPECT – When someone violates health and safety procedures, do you talk to them in private? Before calling someone accident prone, ask yourself did you provide the necessary communication and training to do the job safely. Did you consider what crossroad this individual was at? Have you looked at other contributing factors? Ask open-ended questions without blaming, judging or instilling fear. Be cautious of body language and tone when asking questions. Remove the *Bully* attitude. Take mutual responsibility without name calling or assuming they are at fault.

➤ TRUST – As mentioned above, do you build trust where you follow through on health and safety concerns? Is there consistency with employees, removing favoritism? Do you keep your promises? People will come to you with their concerns if they feel they can trust you. They need to feel comfortable that you are not going to judge or laugh at what they have to say. They need to know you will address the problem; otherwise there is no sense in coming forward. They need to feel that you value their concerns. They need to know that you respect them and will keep conversations confidential. Building trust builds voice and honesty.

➤ INTEGRITY AND HONESTY – Included in your values should be the importance of integrity and being honest. Your integrity should include caring and ensuring that people don't get hurt. Don't be guilty of putting production and deadlines before the safety of your workforce. Lead by example without double standards. Set expectations with written policies and procedures and remove fear by encouraging the importance of honesty. This is accomplished by letting people know that mistakes happen but dishonesty is not tolerated.

Think of the difference it would make if we encouraged ideas, if we gave people respect and dignity, if we built trust and were honest. Think about how your integrity is viewed when there is dishonesty. These elements are essential when operating at the *Commitment Crossroad*. It is difficult to develop positive relationships without voice, dignity, respect, trust, honesty, and loyalty.

FIFTH TOOL

TEAM-BUILDING

What will you gain from this chapter?

See the coalition when you operate at the "Commitment/Responsibility"
Crossroad.
See what happens when your team interacts in a positive, productive manner.
Recognize what makes a successful team.

SIGNS OF A PROBLEM TEAM MEMBER

1. **On the Beach** – blames, passive, doesn't get involved, doesn't take responsibility in completing tasks.
2. **Bullying** – condescending, puts people down, relays his feelings toward a person by cracking jokes, argues, and is closed-minded to other people's ideas, thinks of himself rather than the team, and is always right.
3. **Complacency** – not willing to change and move ahead.
4. **Firefighter** – doesn't consider all options or take into consideration existing workload and resources needed.

WHAT MAKES A SUCCESFUL TEAM?

- ➤ **Committed** – The team works at the *Commitment Crossroad*, leaving behind obstacles from previous crossroads. The team is in the "here and now," willing to contribute in a positive way.
- ➤ **Voice, dignity, respect, trust and integrity** – The team operates using concepts from the *fourth tool* in their toolkit. The team respects each other's differences while focusing on the problem, not the personality.
- ➤ **Communication** – The use of the *Third Tool* in your toolkit gives the team excellent communications skills, along with the benefits of respect, trust, and encouragement. Effective communication is critical when operating at the *Commitment Crossroad.*
- ➤ **Sharing the workload** – The team is committed and shares the workload.
- ➤ **Supportive of each other** – Team members support each other, acknowledging small successes and helping other members to overcome obstacles.
- ➤ **There is a positive atmosphere** where people enjoy being on the team.
- ➤ **The team is able to resolve conflict** in a positive way without attacking or focusing on the personality.
- ➤ **Negativity, blaming, and judging** are unacceptable and needs to be addressed.
- ➤ **Reaching a consensus** – When making a decision a consensus needs to be reached by the team. You ultimate

goal is to obtain approval from all team members where possible.

➤ **Celebrate success** – The team celebrates when they have accomplished a goal. The team recognizes individuals who have done a good job.

➤ **Committed** – You are present and contribute to the meetings success.

A TEAM APPROACH
IMPLEMENT A POSITIVE HEALTH AND SAFETY CULTURE

➤ A team approach starts with a safety policy that everyone embraces and takes responsibility for.

➤ Senior management and all members of the organization need to be committed from the very start.

➤ Involve staff with hazard-reporting procedures, stressing the importance of everyone taking responsibility in eliminating safety hazards. It is not one person's responsibility to clean up a spill, but whoever sees it needs to clean it up.

➤ Outline roles and responsibilities for managers, supervisors and employees.

➤ Barriers are removed, which in turn eliminates fear.

➤ When someone makes a promise, you follow through with the promise in question.

➢ The Joint Health and Safety Committee are supported by the management team.

➢ The management team follows through on recommendations.

➢ The Joint Health and Safety Committee works with management to eliminate injuries and illnesses in the workplace. A team approach is used removing barriers between employees and management members. When entering a JHSC meeting, your goal is to ensure a safe workplace. Leave your various hats, attitudes, and ego at the door. Enter into an equal playing field where everyone is striving for the same goal. Imagine that you own the business as you work at resolving various problems, taking into consideration safety issues and the business at hand.

➢ The Joint Health and Safety Committee consider various options before making recommendations. They consider the cost, how easy it will be to implement and how successful their recommendation will be if acted upon. They put themselves in the shoes of the owner before making recommendations.

➢ The Joint Health and Safety Committee encourage employees to get involved and provide input. This is accomplished by talking to people as you do your monthly inspections.

SIXTH TOOL

TIME MANAGEMENT
DELEGATION AT IT'S BEST

What will you gain from this chapter?

In our busy world, we have given you some tips toward effective time management.
Learn to delegate effectively, setting the person up for success.
See the advantage of being proactive instead of reactive.
Are you a Firefighter, always putting fires out? What are you going to do to change?

(A) TIME MANAGEMENT

➢ Make up a weekly plan, prioritizing your work according to your goals.

➢ Don't get sidetracked or procrastinate.

➢ Attempt to eliminate double handling as much as possible.

➤ Be organized so you know where everything is. Keep phone calls short and to the point.

➤ Use electronic means of communication such as e-mail. This eliminates the chitchat.

➤ Delegate where possible. Learn to say NO when you are overloaded.

➤ Plan meetings with an agenda sent out prior to the meeting.

➤ Start meetings on time, delegating responsibility while setting timelines for completion.

➤ Take minutes of the meeting, so there is a hard copy of the discussion, action steps, who is going to take responsibility, and what is the specified timeframe to complete the initiative.

➤ Eliminate jokes and junk mail from your e-mail inbox.

➤ Have a parking lot where discussions that are not related to the meeting or are going on too long can be placed and addressed at another time. (*A parking lot is a piece of paper where you place non-related questions that have come to mind through discussion. This allows you to address the item later when there is more time. The issue is not forgotten and it removes the perception of being ignored.*)

➤ Assign responsibilities, timelines, follow-up, and adjournment.

(B) EFFECTIVE DELEGATION

How many of us, especially if we are operating at the *Firefighter Crossroad*, give a task to someone, only to take it back? Our impatience destroys confidence and loyalty with the employee. It also makes the person feel like they have failed and disappointed you. Typically, people want to do a good job and they want to please. You need patience while considering all aspects before handing over the task. Here are a few tips in setting people up for success when delegating:

➤ **Delegate to the person** who has the skills, mental capability, and time to execute the task. Give the person a reason why you are asking them specifically to do the task, so they are committed and excited about the project ahead.

➤ **Delegate the whole project.** This gives the person a feeling of accomplishment, as well as a sense of pride and ownership. This is great for morale.

➤ **Delegate communicating your expectations and when you need it completed.** By placing timelines and why these deadlines need to be met, it holds the individual accountable and gives them a sense of urgency. Assess whether the amount of time is realistic, otherwise you are setting the person up for failure. Remember, each of us has a different learning curve, depending on past experience, knowledge, and cognitive skills. Allow for additional time.

> **Delegate with mutual acceptance and agreement to finish.** Mutually discuss the project to ensure full understanding of expectations and timelines. Consider potential obstacles, removing fear if they hit a roadblock that is preventing them from completing the task at hand.

<u>DO NOT RESCUE – BE PATIENT</u> – Inquire about progress, but give the individual an opportunity to finish what he or she has been assigned. It may take longer the first few times, but once they get the hang of it, they will be able to complete it at a faster pace.

SEVENTH TOOL

HEALTH AND WELLNESS - BALANCING WORK AND HOME
What will you gain from this chapter?

See the effects of stress and the importance of balancing your life at work and at home.

What is the cost of all work and no play?

Looking after your health and well-being is a priority if you are going to reach your goals and perform to the best of your ability. Take time out of your busy schedule and enjoy life. If you base success strictly on your career, then you are missing the boat. Your true happiness comes when you can balance work without compromising your family or health.

STRESS is something that we are facing more than ever in today's world. We may not even realize the amount of stress we are subjecting ourselves to. Some symptoms you may be experiencing are high blood pressure, loss of appetite, overindulging, loss of patience, anxiety, a defensive attitude, depression, digestive problems, or a feeling of helplessness. It is common to take our stress out on the ones we love as a means of venting. This creates another dimension in our unhappy stressful life.

<u>What causes stress?</u> There are a number of reasons for stress. The *Firefighter* pushes the envelope to the point of burnout. Some of us have the unfortunate experience of working in a toxic, negative environment where we hate our work and fear job security. Others are in an environment where *Bullying* is present. Due to downsizing and cutting overhead costs, our workload has increased, resulting in long hours at work. We may also be in a position where the job we are performing is not within our comfort zone. Communication, a lack of caring and respect, low self-esteem, and a feeling of not being appreciated are also contributing factors.

We are faced with all of these issues, coupled with the challenge of juggling home, work, and family. We have the newlyweds who struggle to pay their school loans, get a house, and prepare to have a family. The baby boomers are sandwiched between their children needing financial assistance, staying home longer, and their elderly parents requiring assistance. Credit is easy. People have the attitude of borrowing for today and worrying about paying it later. In paying it back you then find that a huge chunk of your money is spent carrying the interest charges. You haven't even put a dent into the principle. To cope with these stressors, many turn to alcoholism as well as drug and gambling addictions. These pressures are taking their toll as more and more people suffer from depression and emotional disorders, resulting in anti-depressants being used more than ever. Who has time to make healthy home-cooked meals or exercise? You will find that people who exercise have less stress and more energy. They feel better physically as well as emotionally, and yet are too busy to prioritize or put the time aside. Unfortunately, often something needs to happen to us before we take action. We have a heart attack and then we stop smoking, eat differently, and start exercising. Don't wait until something happens. Set your priorities.

ELIMINATING STRESS

1. **Operate at the** Commitment Crossroad, leaving all other crossroads behind.
2. **Choose to be positive** – Be positive and use a "can-do" approach. Don't dwell on "I can't."
3. **Prioritize** and remember one step at a time. Don't try to eat the whole elephant.
4. **What is out of your control,** let go and move on.
5. **Assess what is within your control** and what you need to do to eliminate stress you are experiencing.
6. **Time management** – Don't take on more than you can physically and emotionally handle. Learn to say no. Delegate or get assistance. Realize that you can't make everyone happy.
7. **Set time aside** for vacation, fun, and relaxation.
8. **Continuously learn** how to maintain a balanced lifestyle.
9. **Nutrition** – Start paying attention to your eating habits by making healthy meal choices.
10. **Seek professional assistance** – Get help through your employee assistance program (EAP), your family physician, or other agencies that can assist you through your seemingly impossible roadblocks.
11. **If you hate your job,** outline a plan on how you can move on, finding something that you will enjoy.

12. **If you hate your relationship**, ask yourself why. Mutually work through your obstacles and frustrations. Talk to each other with an open mind, listening without judging.

13. **Exercise** – This may be walking, jogging, swimming, dancing, or joining a sport-related activity. Do stretching exercises to reduce and eliminate strains and sprains. Build core muscles to prevent back injuries. See your physician or a personal trainer who can assist you in this area.

14. **Prevent potential injury and illness** both on and off the job.

15. **Live for today** – We don't know when our number is up. How many people work their whole life without having an opportunity to enjoy it? Don't have regrets when you look back on your legacy.

16. **Build an action plan** – Assess areas where you can improve, both physically and emotionally. Set up a plan of what needs to change for you to feel better.

> Case in Point: *When I first started working, I was the Super Mom. I was attempting to do it all. I was running our daughter to dancing four days a week, coupled with hockey practice, as well as keeping the house as clean and organized as before. I was making all of my own clothes, drapes, bedspreads, as well as helping my husband with bigger projects. During that time, we had both gone through surgery.*
>
> *My boss asked me to do something, which resulted in me breaking down into uncontrollable tears. I soon realized I had to make time for me and start giving up some of the tasks that I was so used to doing. I couldn't do it all.*

<u>Case in Point:</u> *I remember when my husband had a brain tumour; we vowed we would change our lifestyle. His prognosis was dead, blind, or crippled. Living normally was not in the cards. I must say that we were fortunate, as he came out of the operation with flying colors. He went back to work five months later and has been well ever since. This was our wake-up call. Life is short, so make the most of the time you have. We vowed we would always take a vacation. We prioritize quality time together for leisure activities. We make time for our family and friends. We attempt to eliminate unnecessary stress where possible.*

PROMOTING HEALTH AND WELLNESS AT WORK

- ➢ Assess your employee's workload before dumping more work on them.
- ➢ Encourage healthy menu choices in cafeterias and vending machines.
- ➢ Encourage going to the gym or doing lunch walks.
- ➢ Set up lunch-and-learns on various topics.
- ➢ Ensure that people take their vacation.
- ➢ Provide daycare on the premises.
- ➢ Set up an Employee Assistance Program (EAP).
- ➢ Encourage people to use their healthcare benefits, e.g., massage therapy.
- ➢ Bring fitness consultants in to assist employees with a healthier lifestyle.
- ➢ Implement stretch programs to reduce the risk of strains and sprains in the workplace.
- ➢ Provide additional personal days over and above vacation days.
- ➢ Think of ways to reduce unnecessary stress in the workplace.
    - o Effective delegation without overloading
    - o Encourage people to balance work and home
    - o Do fun activities with your staff
    - o Make people laugh

EIGHTH TOOL

EFFECTIVE COACHING

What will you gain from this chapter?

See how you can influence and help people reach their goals through "effective coaching."

Effective coaching is an art that will be part of your legacy that you leave behind. I have been extremely fortunate to have two professional coaches in my life.

At Home

Whether we realize it or not, we are a coach and mentor to our kids, family and friends alike.

> Case in Point: *Many evenings, I would be sitting with my best friend, going over the pros and cons of a decision I needed to make. She is a special friend, in that she listened to what I was attempting to figure out and then we would talk openly about the best approach. She voiced her opinion in a gentle way, giving her take of the situation, but not making me feel I needed to do it "her way." By speaking out loud, I was able to digest what needed to be done and do it. Her questions helped in making the right decision.*

I think we sometimes get caught up as the rescuer, when all the person wants is someone to voice their frustrations or problems to. They want someone to listen to them without judging or pushing their opinion. If you are a high achiever, you will tend to expect other people to think and operate like you do. This is when patience and stepping back comes in, as you realize everyone's makeup is different. Your internal motivation isn't necessarily the same as someone else's. It is easy to provide an answer to a problem and be perceived as knowing it all. It is sometimes difficult to be humble, fearing you will not be needed or jealous that the person may surpass you. Your job is to encourage people to learn by making their own decisions through identifying various solutions, and in some cases making a mistake. The key is to let them know that making a mistake isn't the end of the world, as long as they learned a valuable lesson that won't be repeated. Through this whole process, you are building a relationship of trust, respect, and loyalty, as you continue to coach and mentor people around you. This comes back time and time again, as they want you to be proud of them. They don't want to disappoint you, and will do anything it takes.

Our environment is filled with what we can't do, instead of what we can do. We are subjected to negativity in all phases of our life. Success is the result of never giving up, being internally motivated, and having someone who is there to encourage you. Success is when we can balance our career and private life. As a coach, you are the emotional supporter when there is self-doubt. As a coach, you keep us on track, helping us realize there is light at the end of the tunnel.

At Work

Remember your "legacy." How will you be remembered? Your job is to take the diamond in the rough and make it shine. Your coaching, mentoring, enthusiasm, and support will help the person grow past their comfort zone. Whether you are a manager, supervisor, or co-worker, your influence in someone's life can lead them down a path they never thought they would go. Enthusiasm and passion are contagious. Inspire someone you know to grow beyond their expectations.

Case in Point: *I have been fortunate to attract professionals, family, and friends who have supported and encouraged my endeavours. These people have been instrumental in my emotional growth. Without their support as I stepped out of my comfort zone, who knows what I would be doing today? On the flip side, I have spoken to numerous people who received no emotional support. They either gave up what they were doing or were unhappy because they were always second-guessing whether they made the right decision. They didn't have the luxury of being blessed with positive affirmation that they made a good choice.*

Case in Point: *I had the pleasure of coaching a student who was doing a work term as part of obtaining her diploma in human resources. When I first met her, she was outgoing but hesitant. Through numerous coaching sessions and giving her various projects, I watched her blossom. When we were involved in our first meeting with a third-party individual, she was shy and unsure. Three months later, we met this individual again. Wow, what a transformation. I watched with pride as she answered questions with confidence. When the individual left, I couldn't contain my excitement in sharing how she performed. She told me later that before we had gotten together she wasn't excited about doing HR. I helped breathe life into human resources and health and safety as she shared my enthusiasm. She learned from me but most importantly, she built her confidence up by taking on various projects.*

TIPS ON COACHING

Your job is to coach, mentor, inspire, listen without judging, and encourage.

Don't give up when you think it is impossible.

> ➤ Ask for solutions, not problems,
> ➤ Refer to the *Fourth Tool* – voice, dignity, respect, trust, and integrity.
> ➤ Encourage learning – training and positive affirmation statements.
> ➤ Spend time with your people, listen, encourage, and keep your promises.
> ➤ Be compassionate and understanding and maintain confidentiality.
> ➤ Be positive, clear, concise, and non-judgmental, be a sounding board without judging.
> ➤ Build on people's strengths to reach their full potential.
> ➤ Coach on areas they need to improve on. Determine if they are in the right job.
> ➤ Facilitate learning with a "can-do" approach.
> ➤ Share knowledge without being threatening or condescending.

- Provide clear direction with specific, measurable, achievable, and realistic goals.
- Most of all, set goals that can be reached, taking into consideration their workload, cognitive understanding, and physical capabilities.
- Instead of telling, ask questions – get them to take ownership.
- Encourage people to learn from their mistakes.
- Reward performance with incentives or an appreciation program.
- Thank the person and acknowledge when the person has done a great job.
- Determine financial rewards and incentives, tying them to a formalized performance appraisal.

A good boss who is confident within himself or herself will encourage someone to the point of being able to move on or take his/her job. If you have planned effectively, you will be able to move on and make a difference somewhere else. It is all about attitude and how we look at life.

EIGHTH TOOL

EFFECTIVE COACHING - HEALTH AND SAFETY

- ➢ Praise and acknowledge when people follow safe operating procedures.
- ➢ Acknowledge when someone goes out of their way to eliminate hazards.
- ➢ Encourage employees to work safely without taking shortcuts.
- ➢ Encourage employees to identify solutions when they have safety problems.
- ➢ Continue to observe and coach employees after initial training.
- ➢ Remove fear so employees will communicate concerns or ask questions.
- ➢ Silence = Permission – When procedures are not being followed, coach the individual with a warning of future consequences if the unsafe practice continues. Saying nothing gives the person permission to continue performing an unsafe practice.

NINTH TOOL

PERFORMANCE FEEDBACK

What will you gain from this chapter?

Understand the importance of continual performance feedback, both informal and formal.
See the benefits for an employee or your family members when you praise a job well done instead of criticizing.

PURPOSE OF PERFORMANCE FEEDBACK

Performance feedback is something that is done on a day-to-day basis throughout the year. The formalized appraisal gives you an opportunity to discuss strengths, areas of improvement, and develop an action plan for the employee's success. It is also an opportunity to look at promotion, raises, or bonuses for a job well done. There should be no surprises when you conduct your formal appraisal. Do you find that you are quick to criticize and slow to reward or provide positive feedback?

Performance feedback encourages a positive behavior and gives an individual an opportunity to improve, instead of being terminated without understanding what went wrong. People typically want to do a good job and want to please. If you are operating at the *Commitment Crossroad*, you will look at the performance appraisal as an opportunity to improve and grow. Is this an area that you can improve on in both your personal and professional life?

BENEFITS OF PERFORMANCE FEEDBACK:

➢ Encourages good behavior while recognizing contributions.
➢ Acknowledges strengths and areas of improvement.
➢ Reviews expectations against tasks performed.
➢ Addresses future promotions and advancement as well as training opportunities.
➢ Builds employee's self-confidence and commitment.
➢ Provides open communication with positive feedback, reviewing expectations against tasks performed. We talked about this in the goal-setting section.

> Case in Point: *As I talked to a general manager of a big-box store, he indicated that it was performance appraisal time. My comment was that he had a big job ahead. His answer was, "No, it isn't a big deal." He then went on to tell me that his employees knew exactly where they stood before their formal year-end appraisal. He had coached and provided both positive feedback and areas that required development. He recognized and let people know at the time if they were doing a good job or if there were areas they needed to improve on. He provided additional training and coaching if they were having difficulties with certain aspects of their job. He had a disciplinary process to go through if the undesired behavior needed to go past an initial coaching session. The year-end appraisal was a review of the past year's achievements as well as areas that still needed to be worked on. It gave an*

*opportunity for the manager to formally recognize
their progress and set up a plan for improvement.
This time would be spent on addressing future career
options and what the employee's goals would be for
the coming year. If available, it is also a time to
provide monetary recognition through raises and
bonuses.*

Case in Point: *Another case came up where another
manager did a performance appraisal with an
individual, letting them know there would be
no monetary compensation due to the company's
financial picture. The manager was apprehensive,
as he felt that a raise would be expected. He couldn't
believe the outcome. The employee thanked him and
told him it was the first time that anyone had taken
the time to let him know how he was doing. People
like to be appreciated and praised for a job well
done. Monetary recognition is only a small part of
the appraisal.*

CONDUCTING A PERFORMANCE APPRAISAL – The purpose is to acknowledge a job well done, as well as correcting performance issues that are preventing the individual from being successful.

- ➤ There needs to be mutual commitment with trust and respect.
- ➤ It is important to be supportive and respectful, focusing on the problem, not the person.
- ➤ You need to be open-minded, non-judgmental, objective, and consistent.
- ➤ It is important to eliminate personal bias or discrimination that can cloud the issue.

- When talking about performance issues, you need to outline specific incidents.
- Use appropriate body language while being an effective listener, being tactful and fair.
- Stay calm while mutually developing a plan of action to improve.

NINTH TOOL – PERFORMANCE FEEDBACK HEALTH AND SAFETY

- "What gets measured and rewarded gets done"[6] If there are no consequences or acknowledgements, then there is no reason to change.
- Include health and safety when offering bonuses, incentives, or raises. Tie these incentives to your annual or bi-annual performance appraisal, the same as you would for meeting operational objectives.
- Silence = Permission – Do not ignore unsafe behaviors; otherwise you are condoning or allowing the undesired behavior.
- Include specific health and safety objectives in performance appraisals, ensuring employees understand their joint responsibility in keeping their workplace safe.
- As a manager, you should observe and walk around giving people an opportunity to ask questions or voice concerns. This also gives you an opportunity to correct unacceptable practices.

---

[6] By Dan Peterson in his book Safety by Objectives.

STEPS TO ENSURE AN EMPLOYEE'S SUCCESS

When there are performance issues, the process is similar, whether the issues are human resource or health and safety related. Have you done everything you can to ensure the success of your employees? Outlined below is what I believe needs to be in place for success:

> ## STEP 1 – MANAGEMENT COMMITMENT
>   - o   To ensure an employee's success, it starts with hiring the right person with the skills, knowledge, and ability to perform the job.
>   - o   Challenge the employee who is overqualified or eager to learn to keep him or her motivated.
>   - o   Be prepared to offer additional training for the person who lacks the qualifications and experience you need.
>   - o   Create a positive, friendly environment where it is easy to communicate concerns and questions without feeling stupid or fearing repercussions.
>   - o   Be visible and approachable - Observe work being performed. Praise a job well done or coach where improvements need to be made.
>   - o   Ensure that management and supervisory staff is trained on giving positive feedback.
>   - o   Ensure that the employee knows the physical demands of the job, to minimize potential injury.

> **STEP 2 – SET EXPECTATIONS THROUGH WRITTEN POLICIES AND PROCEDURES**
> – Do you clearly communicate goals, objectives, policies, and procedures? Do you have job descriptions and safe operating procedures? Have you set performance standards that can be measured so there is no question on what an individual's expectations are? Do you have a health and safety handbook outlining your expectations when it comes to health and safety?

> **STEP 3 – YOUR EXPECTATIONS ARE COMMUNICATED** – Have you communicated policies, procedures, and health and safety expectations? Don't wait for the performance appraisal to address problems. Address problems and give positive reinforcement when the opportunity presents itself. Build a culture where individuals feel comfortable voicing concerns or asking questions.

> **STEP 4 – TRAINING** – Select the method of training. This may include classroom followed with practical on the job training to ensure understanding. Your goal is to ensure the employee thoroughly understands your expectations to perform their job and the importance of working safe. It is very important to let the person know that you are open to questions or concerns at any time. This is where continued coaching and observation comes in.

> Case in Point: *I was flown to British Columbia for People Soft Training. The program was put on my computer eight months later. I remembered the Rocky Mountains, but how to use the program was*

long gone from my memory. Allow for practical application soon after theory training. This will help reinforce the learning that has taken place.

➢ **STEP 5 – EVALUATE METHOD AND SUCCESS OF TRAINING** – Evaluate through observation and additional coaching whether the exchange of information during the training session was understood.

➢ **STEP 6 – ACCOUNTABILITY THROUGH SETTING OBJECTIVES** – Does the individual understand his/her performance and health and safety expectations? Are you conducting a formalized performance appraisal, which will include future promotions, raises, bonuses and/or incentives based on performance, health and safety and meeting objectives?

➢ **STEP 7 – PRACTICAL REINFORCEMENT OF LEARNING** – Have you allowed for practical application and acknowledged a job well done or coached areas requiring improvement.

➢ **STEP 8 – PROGRESSIVE IMPROVEMENT** – Better known as "progressive discipline," it should be "no surprise" if you have coached, mentored, communicated, and trained an individual. You should be addressing performance issues on a day-to-day basis as you observe their performance. It is also important to show your appreciation and give credit for a job well done. Remember when doing a *Progressive Improvement Plan* the progression needs to be focused on the specific undesired behavior. Don't clump two or three different issues together. e.g. don't give a written warning for being late, a one-day suspension for health and safety, and a two-day suspension for quality issues. These are three distinct areas that should have their own line of progression to improve. Your purpose is to change an undesired behavior, so clumping two or three different behaviors together defeats its purpose.

> **STEP 9 – POSITIVE FEEDBACK AND REWARDS**
This is accomplished through observing and providing positive feedback or rewards on a regular basis. You should also implement a formalized performance appraisal semi-annually or annually. This gives you an opportunity to praise a job well done or correct areas that need improvement. Include incentive or bonus programs to reinforce "what's in it for me."

STEPS TO TAKE WHEN CONDUCTING A PERFORMANCE APPRAISAL

I.   Create a Positive Environment

a. Put the employee at ease, ensuring privacy with no interruptions.

b. Let the employee know you are committed to their success. In order for this to happen, you want to provide positive feedback and areas for improvement.

II.   Compare Findings

a. This is done by both the manager and employee filling out a performance appraisal form in pencil. They later discuss their findings. Surprisingly, the employee often tends to be harder on themselves than the manager conducting the performance appraisal.

III.   **Talk about Accomplishments**
   a. Discuss strengths, accomplishments, and expectations met.
   b. You are giving praise for accomplishments achieved.

IV.   **Acknowledge a Job Well Done** through a thank you, incentives or pay increases.

V.   **Talk about Areas of Improvement**
   a. Do not talk in terms of mistakes, fault-finding, or pre-judgments.
   b. Refer to specific times and situations. This should come to no surprise because you have already given them this feedback when it happened.
   c. Take responsibility to determine if there is something the management team could have done better. e.g. training, coaching, or more time to grasp the concepts.
   d. Look at the situation optimistically as an area to improve on.

VI.   **Mutually Agree on What Needs to Change, Coupled with an Action Plan**
   a. Agree on targets/goals to be met. Be specific on those goals.
   b. Set deadlines for corrective action.

VII. Summarize and Confirm Understanding

a. Summarize the accomplishments and areas of improvement.

b. Let them know you are available if they have questions or concerns.

c. Reassure the employee you are looking out for their best interest.

VIII. Follow Up

a. Set up a follow-up date to discuss progress or a further plan of action.

b. Continue to coach and observe, making adjustments where needed.

c. Give credit when you see improvements.

IX. Future Goals - The purpose is to uncover their passion.

It may be something that is transferable, which can be utilized within the organization. If not, then you have mentored someone to reach their dream or the next phase of their career. I have also opened a door of communication as I show genuine interest in what they want in life.

> Case in Point – *I was being paid as a contractor, not an employee and yet the Director did a performance appraisal on me. She told me, I was quick at picking up new concepts and then asked what my goal was over the next few years. My response was, "I wanted to write a book. This had nothing to do with the employer I was contracting with, but it gave me a great deal of admiration that she would take time out of her busy schedule to conduct a performance appraisal and ask me about my future endeavors.*

TENTH TOOL

PROGRESSIVE IMPROVEMENT PLAN (PIP)
Better Known as Progressive Discipline

What will you gain from this chapter?

Understand the importance of setting standards and holding people accountable for their actions.
Understand how to discipline with the goal of changing a behavior and keeping retention.

If we look back in time, disciplinary action meant building a file so we could terminate the employee. This philosophy has changed. The object of disciplinary action is to identify an undesired behavior or performance issue and mutually agree on a plan to correct it. Many of us call the process "disciplinary action" or "progressive discipline." I choose to call it a progressive improvement plan. The name speaks for itself. Our goal is to address performance issues.

Why Employees Win Wrongful Dismissal Suits

➢ Failure to communicate clearly your expectations on the job requirements.
➢ Failure to provide and ensure an understanding of policies and procedures.

- ➢ Failure to implement a formalized process to correct the undesired behavior.
- ➢ Failure to be consistent throughout the operation.
- ➢ Condoning performance issues by warnings with no real consequences.

Progressive improvement should be minimized if everyone is operating at the *Commitment Crossroad.* As mentioned in the previous chapter, our job is to set the person up for success in the beginning. Outlined below are steps to take when coaching an individual through a PIP.

- ➢ **Step 1** – Before we blame the employee for not meeting expectations, it is important for us to take responsibility. Was the employee aware of your expectations? Refer to "Steps to Ensure an Employee's Success" in the previous chapter. This, coupled with effective listening, communication, and training, as well as being consistent in letting people know where they stand, is extremely important. We need to assess whether we have set the person up for success in the first place.

- ➢ **Step 2** – Problem-solve to determine why the situation came up.
  - Be specific on the undesired behavior and the reason why it is not acceptable.
  - See if there is something you could have done to set the individual up for success.
  - Let them know that you value them as an employee and want them to succeed.

- Has the undesired behavior been an accepted practice by others?
- Establish whether the employee has the physical and cognitive skills.
- Refer to the employee's past record and documented conversations and meetings.

➢ **Step 3** – Complete a Progressive Improvement Plan with the employee, outlining his commitment to change. (The violation must be based on the same infraction when progressing to the next step. You are correcting a specific behavior, e.g. lateness or health and safety.)
- A description of the undesired behavior and where improvements need to be made.
- Include an action plan on how the individual is going to change.
- A statement including date, signatures, follow up date and future consequences.

Example of a Progressive Warning –
1) First step – Informal discussion;
2) Second step – Formal verbal warning;
3) Third step – Written warning;
4) Fourth step – One to three day suspension followed with termination.

TIPS IN CONDUCTING A PROGRESSIVE IMPROVEMENT PLAN

1) **Discipline in a private area** – Disciplining in the open is humiliating, embarrassing, and disrespectful. Keep the person's dignity intact. If you are correcting an undesired behavior, take the person into a private area so there is no embarrassment.

2) **Discipline close in time** – The undesired behavior needs to be addressed at the time it happens. If you are training your pet dog, you discipline or praise at the specific time you see it happen not after the fact. The same thing holds true with people.

3) **SILENCE = PERMISSION** – Don't overlook violations. Silence is the same as giving permission for the undesired behavior, hence the undesired behavior continues. Give the individual the benefit of the doubt, coaching and talking to them about the behavior you expect. Let them know that if their behavior continues in a negative way, you will have no choice but to take progressive disciplinary action.

4) **State your expectations in a positive manner** and why it is important to meet these expectations. What is the benefit to them, their customers, and the organization?

5) **Be fair** – You will be respected if you are fair. Avoid favoritism and establish consistencies.

6) **Lead by illustration**. You cannot discipline if you are guilty of the same behavior.

7) **Base discipline on policies and procedures that have been communicated** – Discipline should be based on known expectations that have been communicated.

8) **Base discipline on the undesired behavior, not the person** – Be objective and impersonal.

9) **Consistency** – You must be consistent throughout the organization. All managers and supervisors need to operate at the same crossroad of commitment.

10) **Never lose control**. It is essential that you maintain self-control. Be calm and refer to the section on conflict management. You become a role model for others. Don't jeopardize your relationship and lose respect among your colleagues because you cannot handle and defuse a situation.

11) **Be honest** – Be open, honest about the seriousness of the infraction.

12) **Don't judge** – Don't judge the employee on your perceptions.

13) **Don't fall into** Bullying – Your goal is to assist the employee in recognizing and eliminating the undesired behavior in a positive manner.

14) **Establish a consistent** Progressive Improvement Plan – By doing this, there are no surprises. Employees know what is coming, and the punishment is the same across the board. This removes favoritism and lack of consistency.

15) **Stay out of the employee's private life** – Your concern is addressing what the individual is not doing once they are on your premises.

16) **End on a Positive Note** – Let the employee know you value them as an employee and want them to be a successful part of the team.

Part III

DUE DILIGENCE

<u>WHAT IS DUE DILIGENCE?</u> – Due diligence is the level of judgment, care, prudence, determination, and activity that would reasonably be expected to exist or occur under particular circumstances. Have you taken every reasonable precaution in the circumstances to protect the worker? If your answer is "no" and you live in Ontario, you could be faced with the following penalties.

In Ontario, Canada, the government has taken a strong position in eliminating injuries and illnesses in the workplace by implementing fines and penalties both federally and provincially. An organization can be federally charged under the Criminal Code or provincially charged individually and as a corporation. The provincial government in the past couple of years has increased their inspectors to enforce legislated responsibilities. They have also initiated on-the-spot ticketing, where inspectors have been advised to hand out individual tickets to employees when they observe unsafe practices or non-compliance issues. If there are no procedures or training in place, the ticket will go to the owner or supervisor, depending on who is deemed at fault. Non-compliance issues will result in written orders with potential fines and penalties.

WHY ORGANIZATIONS ARE PROSECUTED FOR VIOLATIONS

Unfortunately, sometimes an individual or an organization needs to be fined, penalized or an individual goes to jail before they look at health and safety differently. There is always *The Magic Thought – Can't Happen to Me.* It couldn't possibly impact my business or me personally. The perception is that these laws are designed for everyone else. These companies are willing to gamble that nothing will happen. It goes back to T*he Magic Thought – Can't Happen to Me.*

Even with fines, penalties, and additional enforcement, organizations continue to take shortcuts and circumvent their required duties. If hitting their bottom line gets their attention, then that seems to be the road to take; otherwise everything remains the same. They will prosecute those people who violate regulations, who have repeat occurrences, who are responsible for critically injuring or causing death resulting from not taking every reasonable precaution to protect the worker.

The purpose of prosecution is to change *The Magic Thought.* As a company, you have *The Magic Thought* that you can ignore legislated requirements and nothing is going to happen to you personally. The reality is that until someone reaches into your personal pocketbook, nothing will change. This forces individuals to realize the consequences when health and safety is ignored.

An example of being due diligent is your ability to prove that you have taken every reasonable precaution to protect the worker from potential injury or illness. Consider the following:

- An organization that operates at the *Commitment Crossroad*.
- An organization that is aware and complies with their legislated responsibilities.
- An organization with written policies and procedures that have been communicated.
- A health and safety policy taken seriously and supported with a health and safety system.
- An organization where the Internal Responsibility System is embraced by everyone.
- An organization who has implemented a continuous improvement plan.
- An organization who has the ability to prove they have done "everything reasonable" to protect the worker.
- An organization that holds people accountable through performance feedback and progressive discipline when procedures are not adhered to.

BENEFITS OF A POSITIVE HEALTH AND SAFETY CULTURE

It is estimated that workplace injuries cost an organization ten times the initial cost of lost time wages and medical treatment. Some of these costs come from the need to hire replacement staff, the cost of additional training, time to conduct a thorough accident investigation, morale, customer service, and administration costs. Some of the benefits when you foster a positive health and safety culture are as follows:

- ➢ Increased morale, as everyone cares and looks out for one another. People feel appreciated.

- ➢ Blame and negativity is not acceptable as people operate at the *Commitment Crossroad*.

- ➢ A team approach, where everyone works together in creating a positive health and safety culture.

- ➢ The Internal Responsibility System becomes part of doing business when everyone takes responsibility.

- ➢ Everyone works toward the vision and mission of the organization.

- Accidents, property damage, injuries, and illnesses are eliminated.

- Employees stay in *Phase Two* when they are motivated and competent.

- Fines and penalties by government agencies are eliminated.

- Elimination of pain and suffering, along with life altering changes.

- Elimination of direct and indirect costs of hiring, training, recruiting, absenteeism, and down time.

- Employees communicate openly without fear of consequences.

- Increased energy by encouraging a healthy lifestyle.

- The Joint Health and Safety Committee are effective in recognizing, accessing, and recommending controls.

- Recommendations are acted upon.

FIRST KEY ELEMENT

LEADERSHIP COMMITMENT IN HEALTH AND SAFETY

Through Your Health and Safety Policy

<u>Health and Safety Policy-</u> A health and safety policy is a letter written by the owner, CEO or senior management member. It is signed, dated and posted on your bulletin board. This policy outlines leadership commitment but also includes the necessity that supervisors and employees be equally committed in eliminating injuries and illnesses. Include in your policy your personal commitment in meeting legislative compliance. Outlined below are some further considerations to support your health and safety policy.

> - Are people at all levels of the organization operating at the *Commitment Crossroad* where barriers have been removed?
> - Are you committed to acting on recommendations and suggestions?
> - Do you have a budget for health and safety?
> - Is health and safety treated the same as meeting quality, health standards, production quotas and customer service standards?

- ➤ Have you communicated the importance that you need everyone's commitment to foster a positive health and safety environment? You can't do it alone.
- ➤ Do you encourage teamwork and empower people to get involved?
- ➤ Are you fostering the importance of being healthy and safe 24/7?
- ➤ Do people voice their concerns without fear of repercussions?

As you can see, your health and safety policy goes beyond a letter posted on the bulletin board. If you want to breathe life into your health and safety policy, you need a health and safety system that supports your commitment. You can't expect people to climb aboard without being coached and shown the way. Include health and safety into your "vision" and "values" while communicating to people that there is no such thing as *The Magic Thought – Can't Happen to Me.*

We know that given the right circumstances, an accident can happen, leaving a person with an altered lifestyle. We want people to understand that we care and want them to go home the same way as they came in to work. We want them to realize the importance of their personal commitment to eliminate injuries and illnesses, both on and off the job. This can only be accomplished if the management team has embraced the same philosophy. If hazards are not corrected, if health and safety is jeopardized to meet production quotas, and if there is no budget or commitment, then what you are asking becomes a joke. If you want your employee's commitment, then you need to be equally committed by supporting their endeavors.

<u>Case in Point:</u> *If I told you to get on the bus outside, would you walk out your door and get on the bus? I would be surprised if you didn't first ask, "Where is it going?" If we want to motivate our people to climb aboard, they have to know up front why are we taking the journey and what's in it for them. It is critical that you get employees' buy-in and get them excited about your vision. If you want zero injuries, then people need to see that they are also responsible for making it happen. They need to realize there is no magic thought, because given the right circumstances; any one of us can be injured or worse still, killed. They need a hook where they can see "what's in it for them."*

SECOND KEY ELEMENT

INTERNAL RESPONSIBILITY SYSTEM

<u>INTERNAL RESPONSIBILITY SYSTEM</u> – If we look back into the history of the Internal Responsibility System, we will see that the Ontario government appointed a Royal Commission to investigate a situation where a group of coal miners went on strike due to health and safety concerns in 1974. Dr. Ham chaired the commission, which later became known as the Ham Commission.[7]

After investigation, he came up with a concept called the Internal Responsibility System. He felt that, if workers were going to be protected from health and safety hazards in the workplace, everyone would have to take responsibility. His concept required that employers, employees, and the government needed to cooperate and work together to eliminate injuries and illnesses in our workplaces.

This is also the point in time when Joint Health and Safety Committees (JHSC) were instituted. This would open up opportunities for employees to participate with management in maintaining a healthy and safe workplace. They would be the internal auditors recognizing and making recommendations when they observe unsafe conditions and unsafe work practices. They would be the cornerstone in promoting health and safety in the workplace. Through specific Joint Health and Safety Committee

---

[7] Resources used- Practical Loss Control Leadership by Frank Bird Jr. and George Germain

certification training in Ontario, they have been granted the power to stop unsafe work if three dangerous circumstances exist. They are as follows: (1) a provision of the Occupational Health and Safety Act and Regulations in Ontario is being contravened. (2) the contravention poses a danger or hazard to a worker; and (3) the danger or hazard is such that any delay in controlling it, may seriously endanger a worker. [8] This prevents unnecessary work stoppages, which can be very costly to an organization.

The Occupational Health and Safety Act of Ontario created interlocking responsibilities for the employer/owner, directors, supervisors, employees, and outside contractors. If one party fails to do their part in health and safety, there is a breakdown in the system, causing potential injury.

The Ministry of Labour (MOL) is the governing agent who is responsible for the enforcement of non-compliance issues under the Occupational Health and Safety Act and Regulations. This would ensure that organizations adhere to their legislated responsibilities.

The Internal Responsibility System became the principle behind the Occupational Health and Safety Act (OHSA) in Ontario, Canada. Outlined below is how the Internal Responsibility System is broken down.

> **Internal** means all parties work together to identify and solve problems. Safety cannot succeed unless the employer, supervisor, and employees are committed in recognizing, assessing, and controlling hazards. It requires teamwork.

---

[8] Section 44 (1) Definition of a dangerous circumstances under the OSHA of Ontario

- ➤ **Responsibility** means workers, supervisors, and employers are all held legally accountable for workplace safety. This is where the Ministry of Labour gets involved to ensure compliance through fines and penalties under the Occupational Health and Safety Act in Ontario, Canada.

- ➤ **System** means that health and safety systems are in place. This refers to your policies and procedures. The intent is that health and safety is treated the same as any other part of your business.

ROLES AND RESPONSIBILITIES: If the Internal Responsibility System is going to be effective, it is important to include the roles and responsibilities at each level of the organization. As mentioned in the Performance Feedback section, you cannot hold people accountable unless you have set expectations and standards. Refer to the legislated requirements when developing your roles and responsibilities for the employer, supervisors, and employees. This requires written policies and procedures, communication, training as well as holding people accountable for specific health and safety initiatives. These roles and responsibilities are interlocking in that if the employer, supervisor or worker fails to fulfill their responsibilities, they are leaving themselves and others open to potential injury. Your roles and responsibilities are part of the implementation of your mission or how you intend to eliminate injuries illnesses.

THIRD KEY ELEMENT

RECOGNIZE, ASSESS, AND CONTROL (RAC)

RECOGNIZE – Recognizing hazards can be done in numerous ways. I have outlined a few to consider.

- ➢ Monthly JHSC, supervisory, and management inspections.
- ➢ Use of Senses – Recognize hazards by using your senses.
- ➢ Conduct a job hazard and physical demands analysis to determine hazards and physical requirements on the job being performed.
- ➢ Review your trend analysis where you have identified repeated areas of concern. The information for your trend analysis may be compiled from incident reports, first aid log book, summaries obtained from outside agencies, repeat items from inspections and the list goes on. (*See your thirteenth element regarding trend analysis*)

CONSIDERATIONS WHEN RECOGNIZING HAZARDS

Outlined below are areas you may want to consider when recognizing hazards in your workplace.

<u>(1) Actions of People</u>
- ➤ Do employees put themselves at risk due to good intentions?
- ➤ Has the supervisor made it clear that they must put their health and safety first, making sure there is open communication to ask questions when there are concerns or when employees are unsure of a task?
- ➤ Does the employee have the knowledge and training to perform his/her job?
- ➤ Does the employee have the physical and cognitive capabilities to perform the job? E.g., size, stature, physical fitness, or any pre-existing conditions.
- ➤ Do employees perform unsafe methods due to *Complacency* to get the job done faster?
- ➤ Are the tasks they perform routine and an accepted practice?
- ➤ Are the unsafe practices being condoned?
- ➤ Are people rushing, distracted, taking short cuts or not paying attention to what they are doing?

<u>(2) Chemical</u> – When looking at chemical hazards, ensure people receive generic and specific training in handling, storing, and disposing of chemicals. It is the organization's responsibility to implement controls to protect their employees from chemical and biological agents. This includes providing safe operating procedures and training, as well as WHMIS training in Canada, to enable people to understand chemical hazards. Appropriate labeling and material safety data sheets are also required in your

workplace. I encourage that you instill the importance of working with chemicals safely all the time. The idea is to create a habit and awareness both on and off the job.

(3) Energy – Recognize potential hazards caused by energy. They may be frayed cords, potential pinch or in running hazards caused by stored energy. We readily recognize electrical currents as being an energy hazard, but don't forget that hydraulics and stored energy can also be deadly. Implement a lockout procedure where there is zero energy tolerance before working on moving equipment.

(4) Engineering or Equipment Hazards – When purchasing equipment ensure that it has the necessary guarding and safety devices installed. Machinery should also have regular inspections and preventative maintenance programs in place. It is critical that you have a lockout procedure in place and that anyone performing maintenance or adjusting equipment lock it out before putting themselves at risk. Provide training in both theory and practical, followed up with observation to ensure that your expectations have been understood. This is an area where there is zero tolerance for non-compliance of following proper procedures. There can be absolutely NO shortcuts when working around moving equipment. One mistake can cause amputations and potential death.

(5) Environment has many facets. You may be looking at how weather conditions affect the health and safety of your people. You need to look at protecting your staff from heat stress in the

summer and hypothermia in the winter. Weather conditions also give us slip, trip, and fall hazards. Ensure that you have a program set up to keep your parking lot and walk areas free from snow and ice, as well as extra matting to control potential slip hazards when inside the building. Air quality, chemical hazards, lighting, and cluttered or congested areas are all part of the environmental conditions that pose potential hazards. One other area to consider is whether your culture fosters rushing, taking shortcuts or performing unsafe practices to meet deadlines. Will people speak up when they have a concern or are they afraid of being penalized?

(6) Ergonomic – It is important to make the task fit the person, instead of making the person fit the task. Consider the employees' physical structure compared to their work area. Address the amount of pushing, pulling, lifting, posture, and the amount of time a repetitive task is being performed. Educate employees on the importance of stretching, using correct posture, and taking small breaks when working at something that is repetitive. This may be in the form of rotating tasks so the same body part isn't being put into undue stress. This area has a huge price tag on it, as there are more and more people suffering from chronic illnesses caused from ergonomic factors. The result is time off work or having to modify a person's duties to meet their physical restrictions.

(7) Material Handling – Material handling contributes to a vast amount of injuries and illnesses. It is important to have equipment available to handle heavy or awkward material.

Attempt to control material-handling hazards at the source. This may include looking at alternate packaging or the use of lifting devices. If this is not possible, ensure that people are trained in the proper handling of materials, including safe lifting practices. Encourage stretching and building core muscles to protect their back from potential injury.

(8) Mental and Emotional Stress – With our fast-moving environment, this area is becoming more and more prevalent in workplaces. Preventing mental and emotional stress can be accomplished in a number of ways.

➢ Refer to your *Seventh Tool* on Health and Wellness
➢ Implement a harassment, work rage, violence and sexual harassment policy.
➢ Provide an open door policy and options they may consider to get well.
➢ Assess employees' workload and capabilities before delegating.
➢ Encourage a health and wellness program, including work and home balance.
➢ Provide in-house day care, depending on the size of the company.
➢ Communicate the accessibility of your EAP (Employee Assistance Program), where people have a confidential outlet to assist with problems they cannot get past.
➢ Remove "bullying" from your workplace.

(9) Personal Protection Requirements – Have you addressed personal protection requirements for the job that is being

performed? Are you protecting employees from chemical hazards? Have you considered appropriate footwear, appropriate clothing, eyewear, respiratory equipment, earplugs, etc.? Ensure people are wearing the equipment you have provided.

(10) Physical Hazards – Physical hazards are broken down as follows:

Noise – Assess noise levels to determine risk of hearing loss. Where possible, eliminate the noise through barriers or other means. If this is not feasible, provide hearing protection.

Temperature – This area is always a concern in temperature extremes. It is important to provide training to employees so they understand symptoms of heat exhaustion or hyperthermia as well as prevention measures when working in excessive heat or cold.

Vibration – Vibration can cause circulatory, nerve, and musculoskeletal problems. Consider controls when employees are using equipment that causes vibration.

Radiation – Address the types of radiation and controls.

(11) Purchasing - Involve your Joint Health and Safety Committee when purchasing items that may cause potential harm. Before purchasing equipment, take into consideration whether it meets safety standards in your area. When purchasing workstations and chairs make sure they are adjustable. Include the

people who will be using what you plan to purchase. This helps with buy in plus you can assess whether it will fit the person. Address ergonomic, chemical, personal protection equipment, pinch points on moving equipment and any other aspects that could cause potential injuries or illnesses. Refer to your legislation on pre-start up inspections when purchasing new equipment or making alterations.

(12) Work Practices – This is the process to complete a particular task. Are we asking an employee to rush or operate in a way that could result in an injury? Sometimes *Complacency* plays a big part in potential injuries, as people take shortcuts or don't follow policies and procedures. Their attitude is that they have done it forever without incident, so why change? Assess potential risks at each crossroad. This may uncover potential behavior issues.

ASSESS – Some areas to look at when assessing the hazards are as follows:
1. Assess against government regulations, guidelines and codes.
2. Assess to determine if company policies and procedures are being followed.
3. Assess that you have procedures in place.
4. Assess if your method is the best way to perform a task.
5. Use air monitoring to assess air quality
6. Assess if you have provided appropriate training.

CONTROL – There are three ways to control a hazard. The best way to control a hazard is at the source. This keeps the worker out of danger if the hazard has been removed in the first place.

1. **At the Source** – Eliminate or substitute chemicals that have potential to cause cancer or other terminal illnesses. Set up a workstation to fit the person not the person to the task.

2. **Along the Path** – This may be done through engineering or administrative controls, e.g., barriers; vacuum instead of sweeping, engineering controls or ventilation.

3. **At the Worker** – Provide personal protection equipment for the worker. Provide training and written safe operating procedures, including a sign-off sheet that the person has understood your expectations.

FOURTH KEY ELEMENT

WRITTEN POLICIES AND PROCEDURES

Refer to tips in setting up an effective health and safety system

Companies typically feel they do a good job verbally communicating expectations for health and safety. Unfortunately, in most cases, there is a major deficiency in written policies and procedures. This not only applies to health and safety, but I have found it is a common thread throughout many management systems.

There is no doubt that written policies and procedures take time, knowledge, and energy to develop, not to mention the cost of communicating and training employees on your expectations. Although this is time-consuming to implement, the benefits far outweigh the cost of time and money. You will create consistencies where employees know your expectations and where favoritism is eliminated as everyone is on the same playing field. If you are challenging a legal allegation with a government agency, your success rate will be far greater if you have effective systems in place.

Setting expectations can range from safe operating procedures on specific equipment, injury reporting, accident investigation, fire plan, rights of workers, roles and responsibilities, and other policies and procedures that let employees know what your expectations are. Refer to Appendix A for a checklist on suggested policies and procedures. Having a continuous improvement plan that is updated and acted upon to raise the bar is a key piece to keep your health and safety system fresh and in the forefront. This should be driven from the management team in conjunction with the Joint Health and Safety Committee's assistance. People also need to know where they stand. Refer to the *Ninth Tool* in your toolkit on performance feedback on how to set employees up for success.

FIFTH KEY ELEMENT

INCLUDE HEALTH AND SAFETY INTO YOUR BUSINESS PRACTICES

Health and safety should be included in every facet of your business. Include health and safety in your job descriptions, performance appraisals, orientation, on-the-job training, operating procedures, employee handbook, regular informal and formal meetings, progressive disciplinary policy and budgets.

SIXTH KEY ELEMENT

EXPECTATIONS ARE COMMUNICATED

Refer to your Third Tool on communication for details on effective communication.

Communication and written policies and procedures are probably the two areas that cause the most problems from a due diligence standpoint. When we communicate, it is not enough to say it once and walk away. Be visible and approachable ensuring that safe work practices are being followed. You are required to take every reasonable precaution to protect the worker. This means having written procedures, communicating, and training employees on your procedures and their roles and responsibilities when it comes to health and safety. It is important to have sign-off sheets and a form of testing to ensure that they have understood what has been communicated. You must be in a position where you can prove that they had the training and that they understood. Most of all, DO NOT be guilty of Silence = Permission. This is when you see an unsafe practice and say nothing.

Employees have three rights in Canada as outlined below.

1. **Right to Know** – Employees have the right to know about the hazards in their workplace. By conducting a hazard analysis, you can determine the potential hazards on any

given task. From there, you can implement procedures and appropriate training ensuring the employee understands how to avoid injury due to those hazards. You will want to include specific workplace training including Workplace Hazardous Materials Information System (WHMIS) if you live in Canada. The WHMIS regulations outline the safe handling, storage and disposal of chemicals through labeling, material safety data sheets and worker training. If you live outside of Canada, then refer to your own legislative requirements on the safe handling, storage and disposal of chemicals. Train on policies and procedures including safe operating procedures you have implemented on significant hazards. Communicate your expectations in reporting unsafe conditions or concerns. Ensure the worker has understood your training by providing a means of testing and further observation. Provide sign off sheets to prove you have conducted various training initiatives.

2. **Right to Participate** – Ensure that employees know whom their Joint Health and Safety Committee (JHSC) members are, encouraging them to offer ideas in creating a safe and healthy workplace. Support the JHSC, acting on recommendations made.

3. **Right to Refuse** – Ensure that people know that if they believe something is unsafe, they can refuse to do it without fear of repercussions. There is a penalty if you intimidate or terminate an employee because they refuse to do a job that they believe is unsafe or where they feel they could be injured.

SEVENTH KEY ELEMENT

ACCOUNTABILITY

Refer to your Eighth Tool on performance feedback.
"What Gets Measured and Rewarded Gets Done."[9]

Accountability is extremely important. Unsafe behaviors such as shortcuts, not following specific procedures, or not wearing personal protection equipment will continue if there is no accountability. Include specific health and safety objectives in your formalized performance appraisals at all levels. This sends a clear message that health, safety and wellness must not be jeopardized to meet other goals and objectives. Your Joint Health and Safety Committee can assist in developing these objectives. Supervisors also need to be held accountable for their actions. I would suggest that you include raises, bonuses and perks when objectives are met.

[9] By Dan Petersen- Safety by Objectives

EIGHTH KEY ELEMENT

TRAIN, EVALUATE EFFECTIVENESS AND REINFORCE WITH PRACTICAL APPLICATION

Refer to your Eighth Tool on performance feedback, which gives you further tips in these areas.

TRAINING – Determine whether the problem is a training or non-training solution.

> Assess whether you have procedures in place before you look at training.
> Determine learning objectives.
> Determine the appropriate training techniques. Consider the best approach depending on the audience and information that needs to be transferred.
> Ensure that there is an opportunity to practice what was learned. This should be done soon after the training to reinforce the concepts or theory taken place earlier.
> Observe, continue to coach, acknowledge success, and advise consequences.
> Document all training or informal information sessions, including sign-off sheets and testing.

EVALUATE EFFECTIVENESS– It is your responsibility to determine whether you have given enough training and practical application. Observe and coach to ensure that employees have understood your expectations.

> Case in Point: *When two people from another company died in a confined space, I immediately checked with our people to see if we were providing sufficient training and whether they were fully capable and competent to work in a confined space. I was evaluating whether the training we were doing was sufficient. We were considering cutting confined-space training from three days to one day. After speaking to the employees who went into confined spaces frequently, they all agreed to keep the three days for new people and have a one-day refresher yearly to keep everyone on their toes. I was evaluating with my employees' assistance our current training program.*

REINFORCE WITH PRACTICAL APPLICATION –

Coach while reinforcing safe practices. Allow time for practical application to help reinforce the learning that has taken place. Buddy people up with more experience.

NINTH KEY ELEMENT

PROGRESSIVE IMPROVEMENT PLAN

Refer to your Ninth Tool for additional tips on building a Progressive Improvement Plan – Progressive Discipline.

If there are no consequences, then there is no reason to change. This leaves you wide open for prosecution should something happen. It is imperative that people understand your expectations as well as understanding the consequences when expectations are not met. It is equally important to lead by example. Double standards are not acceptable. You can't penalize someone for performing an unsafe practice when you yourself are guilty of the same thing. When I talk about double standards, it is important to treat everyone the same. Whether the employee is a friend, relative, owner's child or someone of importance within the organization, they should receive the same penalty as someone else. It is important that supervisors throughout the operation stay consistent in following policies and procedures. Nothing is worse than having one manager writing everyone up and the other manager ignoring unsafe practices.

Case in Point: *I have seen on many occasions where buddies, friends and relatives were hired and treated different than the rest. It is critical to treat everyone the same no matter who they are or the position they hold. As I once said to a supervisor who hired one of our kids, "if he steps out of line, treat him the same as anyone else." This applies at home. How many people look back into their childhood and comment how their sister or brother was always favored. You may feel you have done nothing wrong, but people from the outside will have the perception that you are favoring one individual over another.*

SILENCE = PERMISSION – We talked about "Silence = Permission" previously. Whether we talk health and safety or human resources, it is all the same. If you ignore the unsafe practice, saying nothing, the message to employees is "it is okay." It is perceived as condoning the unsafe practice or undesired behavior. Be very cautious, as you can be accused of favoritism or discrimination when you pick and choose who is going to be disciplined.

KEY MESSAGE – Communicate expectations, be consistent, lead by example, no double standards, and implement a progressive discipline approach, as outlined in the chapter on progressive improvement. It will be no surprise when an individual is terminated, as you have done everything you can to make it clear what they have to do if they value their job with your organization.

TENTH KEY ELEMENT

ACKNOWLEDGE A JOB WELL DONE

Refer to your Eighth Tool on performance feedback for additional tips.

Acknowledge a job well done when health and safety objectives have been met. This may include elimination of injuries and illnesses, conducting inspections, eliminating hazards, or going above and beyond to ensure a safe workplace. You set the criteria and determine the reward. Some examples are as follows:

> ➤ <u>Conduct a formalized performance appraisal yearly or bi-yearly.</u> Include meeting health and safety objectives. If these objectives are met, then reward your people. If objectives are not met, then hold back your rewards.

> ➤ <u>These rewards may include an increase in pay, employee incentive programs, bonuses, safety awards, not to mention future promotions.</u> This requires setting expectations with objectives that can be measured.

> ➤ <u>Establish a positive feedback system</u> – Acknowledge a job well done at pre-shift meetings or as you observe someone going out of their way to maintain a safe workplace. This may be a simple thank you. Don't take people for granted.

When you observe someone going out of their way to be safe, acknowledge their efforts.

ELEVENTH KEY ELEMENT

HEALTH AND SAFETY 24/7

The business Case to Invest in Health and Safety Both on and off the job

I had a conversation with a safety consultant who informed me that it was not his responsibility to worry about people once they left their place of employment. I beg to differ. If you are a proactive organization that encourages health, safety, and wellness, both on and off the job, the payback will far exceed the money and time spent. A few of those benefits are as follows:

1. **Builds loyalty, respect, and retention** – We know money is not the key motivator to keep retention. We also know there is going to be a huge shortage in human capital when the baby boomers retire. We are faced with a gap, as the present generation is building their careers instead of their families. For this reason, we must build an organization where people want to stay. Money is secondary, as more emphasis is placed on career advancement, being appreciated, and working in a positive environment. If people feel a sense of belonging and know you care, it makes it difficult to pack it in for another job. Creating a health, safety, and wellness program 24/7 builds a positive culture where health and safety becomes a habit and where

there is respect, loyalty, and a sense that people care about you and your family. This gives people a reason to stay. You give people something more than just a pay cheque.

> Case in Point: *I will never forget when the owner who barely knew me came to visit me in the hospital, bringing with him the best chocolates ever. His schedule was crazy and hectic, but he always found the time to acknowledge me and ask how I was doing when I returned to work. This spoke leaps and bounds about who he was. It showed that he genuinely cared about me. My commitment and loyalty were reinforced over and over.*

> Case in Point: *As I was doing supervisory training, one individual commented how he has stayed with the company all these years because of the owner. The owner's attitude is that the employees who work for her are her family. She has an open-door policy and a down-to-earth approach, where people feel comfortable talking to her about a problem. He knows she cares about each and every one of her employees, and for that reason, it motivates him and others to do their very best so they don't let her down. By the way, this is the same owner who always says she is super fantastic.*

2. **Builds habits** – By encouraging health, safety, and wellness—both on and off the job—it makes people aware of hazards and the necessity of taking precautions 24/7.

> Case in Point: *Over the last few years, I have emphasized through WHMIS training, the importance of handling and storing chemicals safely, both on and off the job. I began this push when office workers thought it was a waste of time to take WHMIS training. Their worst chemical was white*

out as they used to joke. This is when I started to include chemical safety at home as well as at work. I needed a hook, "what's in it for me," so instead of them being bored and not interested, they became involved, sharing their stories and realizing the life-altering injuries that can happen both on and off the job. I wanted them to take precautions all of the time instead of feeling forced into it by their supervisors. When asked at the end of the seminar, "What is the golden nugget you are pulling out of today's course?" their answer was, "It raised our awareness to be safe all of the time even, at home."

3. Injuries Off the Job Cost Money

a. Co-workers are required to pick up the slack taking on some of their workload while they are absent, you may have to hire a replacement

b. Your medical and sick benefit insurance costs will escalate

c. Other team members are emotionally upset when a colleague is injured.

d. There is additional stress for people in their department.

e. Customer relations may be at stake as the person has built solid relations where a customer will only deal with that particular employee.

> Case in Point: *One of our managers was on vacation when he lit his barbeque, only to have it malfunction. He received substantial burns that caused him to be permanently scarred. He was subsequently off work for a length of time. This put additional stress on the rest of the staff to keep everything going.*
>
> Case in Point: *There was another interesting scenario where I talk about someone pouring bleach in their toilet and using another cleaning*

agent to clean the tubs and sinks. They also closed the bathroom door so the fumes would not go throughout the house. This particular individual passed out and was taken to the hospital. One of the participants went home and thought about the story I shared earlier in the day. She realized that she was guilty of the same thing. She would close the door to prevent her cats from coming in as she put bleach in the toilet and continued to clean her tubs and sinks with another chemical. The training that she received was her wake-up call. She had been very fortunate in that nothing had ever happened. Given different circumstances, she could have suffered a life-threatening situation. The training brought to light something that she had never given any thought about. If I had conducted normal, generic WHMIS training without sharing this story, she may not have connected that she was doing something that could be potentially fatal at home.

4. **Pain, suffering, and trauma for the whole family and colleagues at work** – When someone is injured, either on or off the job, it not only affects the injured worker, it affects the whole family and people they work with. The family has to cope with life-changing events. They are burdened both financially and emotionally, as they must make changes in their life due to the injury or illness sustained. Co-workers also feel the impact as they see a member of their team struggling. By encouraging health and safety on and off the job, you are fostering a habit that is shared by everyone. Your goal is to eliminate potential illness and injuries beyond your workers. When a family member is injured or killed, as an organization, you are dealing with the emotional upheaval of the employee who

has their mind on the family member instead of working at their full capability.

5. **Employees' time off to assist family member or self when injured** – Employees take time off when their children are sick. How many days would you take off if your child was critically injured and in the hospital? Work is your last priority at this stage of the game. All the more reason to instill in people the importance of being safe on and off the job.

Health, safety, and wellness are often neglected at home. We have that *The Magic Thought – Can't Happen to Me.* We are our own boss once we step into our private empire. We wear an imaginary coat of armor that makes us invincible at home. There is no supervisor standing over us checking to see if we are wearing our personal protection equipment. How many people do you know that actually read labels or look at safe operating procedures? How many people take the necessary precautions to be safe and healthy at home? This is an area where I think we could vastly improve on.

TWELFTH KEY ELEMENT

JOINT HEALTH AND SAFETY COMMITTEE'S (JHSC) EFFECTIVENESS

In Ontario, Canada, we are required to have a Joint Health and Safety Committee when there are more than twenty employees, when ordered by the Ministry of Labor, or when there are designated substances. This committee is made up of management and elected employee representatives. Their job is to conduct inspections, work with the management team in raising health and safety awareness, as well as making recommendations. They have a list of duties and responsibilities, including participating in certification training so they can assist with work stoppages and work refusals.

The Joint Health and Safety Committee are known as the cornerstone to your health and safety system. They are the liaison between management and employees. They are also your internal auditor, to ensure that your health and safety system is working. The one mistake many employers make is transferring the responsibilities from the management team to the Joint Health and Safety Committee. Remember, they don't have the authority to get things done. They can be your advisory committee, but at the end of the day, the Management Team must act on the deficiencies.

If the Joint Health and Safety Committee (JHSC) are going to be effective, there must be commitment from management where recommendations are acted upon. The committee must be given time to prepare for inspections and meetings. The key to the committee's success is when the management team takes the JHSC seriously, and gives credit for a job well done. This motivates the committee in feeling that they are doing something of value and are appreciated. Provide training and resources for your committee, as they can be of great value in fostering and communicating the importance of working safely.

KEY ELEMENTS FOR A SUCCESSFUL JOINT HEALTH & SAFETY COMMITTEE (JHSC)

> First and foremost, leave politics at the door. Come through those doors without flaunting your power or position. You are all on an equal playing field listening and respecting each other with the goal of eliminating illnesses and injuries.

> Treat your time as if it were your own business.

> Remember what your purpose is. Don't blame or pre-judge.

> Everyone needs to be operating at the *Commitment Crossroad*.

> Members are committed at attending all safety meeting that have been predetermined.

> You have set an agenda including starting and ending time.

> Everyone uses the concepts outlined in *Part II* of your *Toolkit*.

- The JHSC draws from different skills and experiences.
- Everyone uses effective communication skills, focusing on issues and not personalities.
- You listen and encourage participation from all members, helping people grow and learn.
- There is a consensus when making decisions.
- Inspections and meetings are performed followed with recommendations to the employer.
- You promote a healthy and safe environment.
- You obtain management support in addressing recommendations. Their job is to act on those recommendations.
- Co-chairs keep the meeting moving. When topics drag on, assign someone to look into it or put the issue aside to be discussed later.
- Advise the co-chair ahead of time what you wish to bring up for new business. The co-chair will determine if the topics are health-and-safety-related and how many items can be brought forward, taking into consideration time restraints and the number of topics raised by other members.
- Write a clear "terms of reference," including responsibilities and protocol for undesired behaviors. *(this is your job description as a JHSC member)* You can include the following:
    - Purpose of the JHSC
    - Roles and responsibilities
    - Who will assist in the investigation of a critical injury
    - When will you hold safety meetings and inspections? Slot the time in your calendar one year ahead.
    - Outline when the management team is required to get back

to you on your recommendations. In Ontario, Canada they have 21 days according to legislation.

o Outline the selection process for employees, the number of people on the committee, how many will be eligible for specific training.

o Outline the importance of having an agenda sent out before the meeting.

o Outline who will take minutes and how the minutes will be distributed.

o Establish a quorum

REFER TO "ROBERT'S RULES OF ORDER," A BOOK THAT EXPLAINS HOW TO CONDUCT EFFECTIVE MEETINGS.

THIRTEENTH KEY ELEMENT

TREND ANALYSIS

A trend analysis will uncover patterns that, on their own, may not seem to be a problem. In Ontario, you can ask for an annual report from the Workplace Safety and Insurance Board. This will give you an outline of all injuries sustained by employees within your organization requiring outside medical attention. If this is not available, you can devise your own report by tracking on a spreadsheet all first aid, medical aid, lost-time injuries and illnesses. Another area to look at is tracking near misses as well as incidents causing property damage.

This allows you to address the effectiveness of your Internal Responsibility System. This is a proactive way of identifying potential issues that could lead into something more serious. Your spreadsheet will uncover time of year, specific individuals who seem to always have incidents, lack of processes, policies, and procedures, communication, training, and lack of coaching and monitoring. Once you can identify the patterns, you will be able to address the root cause and eliminate it at the source.

> <u>Case in Point</u> - *I have seen a situation where there were numerous back strains at various store locations, only to find out one particular product was creating a problem more than I realized. By looking at the annual summary, I could see that various locations were having the same problem. Without doing a trend analysis throughout our*

operations, I would never have picked up on the
seriousness of the problem.

<u>Case in Point</u> - *When a company started tracking*
Band-Aids being taken from their first aid kit, they
found one particular department to be the cause.
They identified the problem and took proactive
measures. They made sure knives were being kept
sharp at all times. They conducted further training
with the employees to ensure that they were using the
knives properly. They also bought mesh gloves for the
employees to wear.

This particular trend analysis brought forward an issue that was proactively addressed before something more serious happened. At this point, they were looking at small, insignificant cuts. These cuts could have led into blood poisoning or a loss of a finger if the trend was ignored.

A trend analysis gives you an opportunity to recognize, assess, and control future problems. It may uncover the following:

1. A pattern of near misses, first aid, minor and major injuries.
2. Property damage.
3. Patterns of process problems, e.g., rushing, time of day.
4. Patterns of the Internal Responsibility System breakdown.
5. Gaps in training and non-training solutions.
6. Equipment, workstation, people, or hours of work issues.

FOURTEENTH KEY ELEMENT

ACCIDENT INVESTIGATION

The purpose of an accident investigation is to determine the root cause, thereby eliminating unsafe practices or conditions in the workplace. The purpose is not to lay blame or crucify someone for the incident. Your job is to recognize, assess, and control the hazard, eliminating future injures. You are looking for contributing factors not what you know from first impressions.

Before blaming the employee, you want to ask yourself the following questions:
1. Did you provide sufficient training? Was the environment unsafe?
2. Was the employee asked to perform an unsafe practice to get the job done faster?
3. Was the method the employee used wrong?
4. Did the employee have good intentions? Was equipment maintained and guarded?
5. Was the behavior an accepted practice? Remember: silence=permission.
6. Did you provide minimal training with the thought, "Anyone can do this?"

Refer to your *Third Key Element* to assist in recognizing the potential hazard. A thorough investigation identifies these deficiencies, rather than blaming an individual based on first impressions.

ACCIDENT INVESTIGATION PROCEDURES

- ➢ Implement an accident investigation procedure, including documentation to be filled out.
- ➢ Outline procedure for reporting first aid, medical aid, lost time, property damage, and critical injuries.
- ➢ Include the roles and responsibilities of the injured employee, the first-aid person, and the manager, supervisor, or senior management.
- ➢ Include the following:
  - o Outline who is involved, what is involved, and when reports must be completed.
  - o Secure the scene to meet legislative compliance and eliminate potential injury. You also want the scene secured so you can do your own investigation.
  - o Notify the appropriate people, as outlined in your policies and procedures.
  - o Investigate the incident. This will include interviewing witnesses and looking beyond your first impressions as mentioned above. You want to analyze the incident, looking for contributing factors. Your investigation should reveal the underlying cause. Was it an unsafe practice or an unsafe condition?
  - o Your next step is to complete the necessary reports and send them to the people you have outlined in your procedure.
  - o Your final step is to make recommendations to correct the problem.

o   Follow up on your recommendations to ensure corrections have been made.

FIFTEENTH KEY ELEMENT

CONTINUOUS IMPROVEMENT PLAN

A continuous improvement plan helps you raise the bar and continually improve health and safety. It keeps health and safety in the forefront. It also gives you an opportunity to determine budget requirements to accomplish specific objectives. Without a plan of action, there is no accountability to keep the ball rolling. The key to being successful is to follow the goal-setting chapter, so you set objectives that are achievable. It is important to assign specific individuals to complete or look into various initiatives. Without this accountability, it becomes all talk and no action.

TIPS IN BUILDING A HEALTH AND SAFETY SYSTEM RESULTING IN A POSITIVE HEALTH AND SAFETY CULTURE

HEALTH & SAFETY CULTURE	Yes	To Do
Implement the concepts I have shared with you in *"The Magic Thought- Can't Happen to Me."*		
Commitment at all levels – Everyone operates at the *Commitment Crossroad* implementing the various tools in your toolkit.		
A shared vision – You have a positive health and safety culture built on safety first, where accidents are unacceptable. Your vision starts with a health and safety policy signed by the owner or senior person.		
Mission – You have a continuous improvement plan that enables you to work through objectives as you build your health and safety system. You include checks and balances to ensure that your health and safety system is working.		
Strong commitment from the top – The senior management team encourages and supports health and safety initiatives, both financially and emotionally.		
You promote health and safety as being important both on and off the job.		
The organization has fostered a positive health and safety culture through effective communication, trust, and respect. People are motivated and enjoy coming to work.		
Show you care – You listen to employees and the JHSC, acting on their concerns.		

Integrity – You follow through on your promises. Employees at all levels of the organization are respectful, they build trust with one another and they don't judge or make assumptions.		
Health and Safety is included into existing management systems – Health and safety is treated the same as any other part of your business. Examples: job descriptions, performance appraisals, orientation, discipline, budget, operational meetings.		
You have implemented written policies and procedures including setting expectations and making people accountable. Employees understand the importance of reporting unsafe practices and conditions.		
You have created a positive health and safety culture where fear and bullying have been removed and where people will come forward with questions and concerns.		
You provide performance feedback acknowledging a job well done. You praise and reward employees when they go above and beyond your expectations.		
Time and Resources – You give employees, managers, and supervisors the time and resources to implement and maintain health and safety systems.		
You have a budget for health and safety the same as any other part of your business.		
Recognize, assess, and control hazards – As per your *Third Key Element* you make every effort to recognize, assess, and control hazards in your workplace.		
You communicate, train, and evaluate expectations.		
There is a point person who is responsible to implement an effective health and safety system.		

Empower employees – You value employees input on how to improve health and safety.		
The management team continually communicates to its employees, keeping them in the loop of what is happening within the organization and in health and safety. (There is no grapevine means of communicating, as people know where they stand.)		
You take responsibility in identifying contributing factors when conducting accident investigations, instead of judging and calling the person accident-prone.		
The management team conducts inspections over and above the Joint Health and Safety Committee's monthly inspections. Unsafe practices and unsafe conditions are addressed.		
POLICIES AND PROCEDURES		
You have a health and safety management and employee handbook with all policies and procedures to follow.		
Roles and responsibilities have been established at all levels of the organization.		
You have an accident investigation procedure.		
You have completed a job hazard analysis for each job and you have set up safe operating procedures to address potential risks.		
You take immediate corrective action on hazards that could cause an injury or illness.		
You have outlined and provided personal protection, as required making it mandatory to wear.		

Subcontractors must adhere to a subcontractor policy. They must comply with all government regulations and not create potential hazards for themselves or employees working on site. They must also provide the necessary documentation before they start work. This includes proof of qualification, liability insurance and in Ontario, Canada they must show a WSIB clearance certificate showing they have paid their premiums. This is done before they perform work.		
You have material safety data sheets for all chemicals in your workplace.		
You have a fire evacuation plan. You do annual fire drills.		
You have an established a hazard-reporting procedure to enable employees to report unsafe practices and conditions without fear of reprisal.		
You have implemented a hearing protection policy in areas that exceed eighty-five decibels.		
You have considered ergonomic hazards in the jobs being performed. You assess the workstation making sure it has been properly adjusted to fit the person.		
You have a procedure on material handling and safe lifting practices.		
You have a lockout tag-out procedure in place. This is used when equipment is faulty or when maintenance is being conducted where there are in-running hazards or pinch points.		

You conduct WHMIS or chemical training initially and you review the training on an annual basis. You have safe handling, use and storage procedures in place. All materials are properly labeled and have current material safety data sheets accessible.		
You have a housekeeping procedure in place to ensure the elimination of slips, trips, and falls.		
You have a policy to address harassment and violence in the workplace.		
You have an Employee Assistance Program (EAP) to assist employees through personal problems that may be hindering them at work.		
You have people trained in first aid and have first aid stations stocked and regularly inspected.		
You have an injury-reporting procedure, including protocol to follow for critical injuries.		
You have an early-return-to-work program that has been communicated to all staff.		
Employees know their three rights: Their right to know, participate and refuse.		
You familiarize employees with the hazards in their workplace, communicating that if they feel something is unsafe, they have the right to refuse work.		
EQUIPMENT AND PROCESSES		
You have preventative maintenance programs on equipment and processes.		
You address lighting, walkways and structural damage.		
You have a purchasing procedure in place to assess health and safety risks before buying.		
New equipment is inspected for safety standards before being put into operation		

Only trained and competent operators are allowed to operate equipment.		
Pre-inspections are conducted on equipment as per policies and procedures.		
Equipment is guarded against pinch points or safety hazards. Equipment is locked out when guards are removed for maintenance purposes.		
COMMUNICATION		
You have communicated your safety policy, making sure employees understand that they play an integral part in recognizing, assessing, and controlling hazards.		
You have a bulletin board dedicated to health and safety. On this bulletin board, you have posted all the necessary information to meet legislative compliance.		
You communicate your expectations on how to perform a task safely.		
Employees know their responsibilities and consequences when health and safety practices are not followed. Employees are also held accountable for their actions.		
Employees know the procedure for reporting unsafe practices or conditions.		
Employees input is welcomed and acted upon when they raise concerns or make suggestions.		
You have a process in place to address language barriers.		
TRAINING		
Employees receive theory and practical health and safety training on tasks they are required to perform as part of their orientation.		
Health and safety is included in the orientation training for new or transferred employees.		

Employees are made aware of the PPE required when doing specific tasks.		
There is job specific training to familiarize employees with the hazards of their job.		
Employees receive generic and work specific WHMIS or chemical training.		
Employees know what personal protection equipment is required to perform their job.		
There is training on safe work practices including fire extinguisher training.		
You have evaluated the method of training, ensuring that people understand your expectations. You test ensuring the transfer of learning was successful. You continue to observe, coach and buddy up employees after initial training.		
You have specific in-depth training when exposed to significant hazards, such as operating equipment, performing lockout, or working in a confined space, etc.		
You have completed an assessment for designated substances in your area. You have also taken the necessary controls to protect the worker. e.g. asbestos, silica, lead.		
Documentation and sign-off sheets – All training, meetings or informal safety talks are documented and signed off as proof of communication.		
MEETINGS		
Health and safety is included in all management or departmental meetings.		
Health and safety is included in meetings involving employees. This is done through lunch box talks, organized training sessions, or during a one-on-one discussion.		

Employees are kept informed of the status of health and safety.		
DISCIPLINARY PROCEDURES		
Supervisors coach employees before disciplining, to ensure the employee understands your expectations.		
You have a disciplinary procedure, which people are made aware of.		
If health and safety procedures are not being followed, you coach and discipline when the person continues to perform unsafe practices. Unsafe practices are not ignored. Silence = Permission is not acceptable.		
ACCOUNTABILITY		
Supervisors/managers are held accountable for ensuring a safe workplace through informal and formal performance appraisals. Health and safety reflects future raises, bonuses and incentives.		
Supervisors/managers are held accountable to meet the health and safety objectives through annual performance appraisals. Health and safety affects bonuses, incentives, and promotions		
JHSC RESPONSIBILITIES AND INSPECTIONS		
The management team fully supports the JHSC by providing necessary training and by listening and acting upon concerns brought up within twenty-one days.		
You have an effective JHSC who assists in recognizing, assessing, and controlling hazards.		
The JHSC has an inspection checklist and conducts monthly inspections.		

Your terms of reference include a calendar of dates for meetings, inspections, as well as roles and responsibilities, how you select JHSC employee members, and how many people have to be present at a meeting to make a quorum.		
JHSC has determined how they will process recommendations and resolve conflicts.		
The JHSC is included in accident investigations.		
The JHSC assists with work refusals and work stoppages.		
The JHSC conducts thorough inspections in an effort to recognize potential health and safety risks. They also include speaking to fellow employees so they can find out additional information that may not be apparent through a walk-about.		
The JHSC uses a proactive approach in looking at areas of improvement over and above items found on their monthly inspections.		
The JHSC and management team encourage health and safety 24/7 by including off-the-job safety in training sessions or offering educational seminars on healthy living.		
The Joint Health and Safety Committee (JHSC) have received the necessary training to perform their duties as a JHSC. They are included in other training initiatives to assist them in their role as a Joint Health and Safety Committee Member as well as knowing company policies and procedures.		
There is a follow-up process to ensure recommendations have been acted upon.		

Index

This book is available as an interactive facilitated program including numerous exercises and breakout groups.

In Ontario, Canada the last day includes an in depth understanding of our Provincial and Federal Regulations.

Build a Positive Health and Safety System as everyone within your organization takes responsibility for health and safety both on and off the job.

Contact Judy Dulovic
Email: contact@themagicthought.com
(905) 574 1099